Sampler Book 14, Ontario in Colour Photos, Saving Our History One Photo at a Time

Photography by Barbara Raué
©2018

Series Name: Sampler Cruising Ontario

Sampling from Northern Ontario

Each photo I take that precedes a demolition, or a natural disaster such as a tornado or a fire, is meeting this aim of mine of Saving Our History One Photo at a Time. There are more than 100 towns already photographed which you can visit without moving from a comfortable chair in your living room.

Cover: 512 Marks Street South, Thunder Bay, Page 37

©All the photos in this book have been taken with my cameras. I own the rights to them.

Table of Contents

Sault Ste. Marie, Ontario – My Top 7 Picks

Lake Superior, Wawa, Dryden, Kenora, Ontario – My Top 8 Picks

Thunder Bay, Ontario – Part 1 – Port Arthur - My Top 12 Picks

Thunder Bay, Ontario – Part 2 – Fort William -My Top 19 Picks

Sudbury, Ontario in Colour Photos – My Top 4 Picks

North Bay, Ontario in Colour Photos – My Top 11 Picks

Parry Sound, Ontario in Colour Photos – My Top 11 Picks

Sault Ste. Marie, Ontario – My Top 7 Picks

Sault Ste. Marie is a city on the St. Marys River close to the US-Canada border. To the south, across the river, is the United States and the city of Sault Ste. Marie, Michigan. These two communities were one city until a treaty after the War of 1812 established the border between Canada and the United States in this area at the St. Mary's River. Today the two cities are joined by the International Bridge. Shipping traffic in the Great Lakes system bypasses the Saint Mary's Rapids via the American Soo Locks, the world's busiest canal in terms of tonnage that passes through it, while smaller recreational and tour boats use the Canadian Sault Ste. Marie Canal.

Before there was a Soo Locks, the place we call "the Sault" was a land covered by trees. The people living in this place called themselves "Anishinabeg," which means "The People." They were Woodland Indians whose homes, clothing, food and tools were all made from the plants and animals they found in the woods and water around them. Where the Soo Locks are today, the river that we now call the St. Marys had huge rocks scattered across it.

French colonists referred to the rapids on the river as *Les Saults de Ste. Marie* and the village name was derived from that. The rapids and cascades of the St. Mary's River descend more than twenty feet from the level of Lake Superior to the level of the lower lakes.

Each spring several large canoes paddled by men from the Montreal area called voyageurs came to the Sault from Montreal. With the voyageurs, came traders from the large fur companies of Montreal and tons of goods to be traded for the furs that the Chippewas had trapped during the winter. Among the trade goods were guns, metal knives and traps, pots and pans, blankets, beads and cotton material. Beaver furs were used to make fashionable men's hats in Europe.

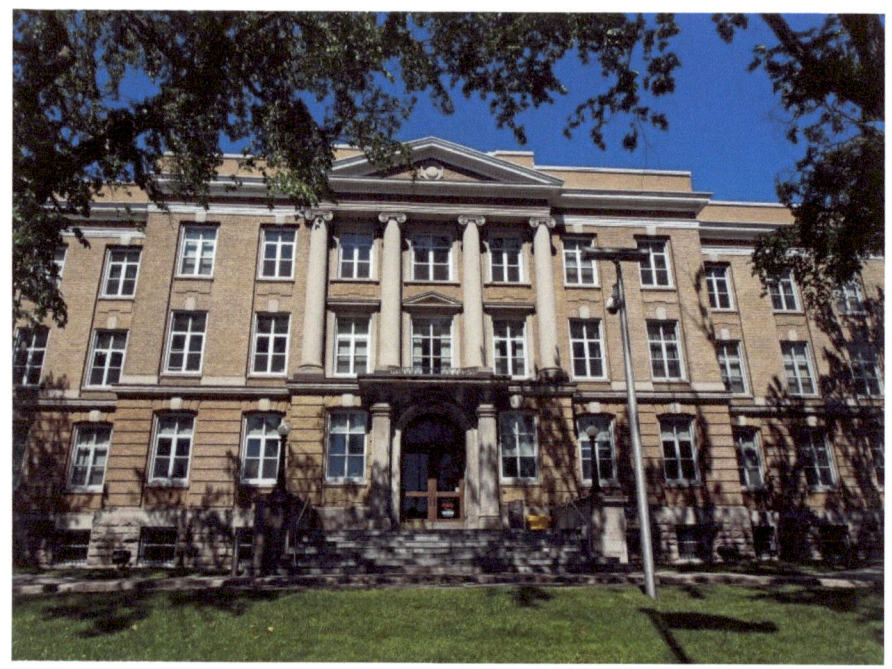

420 Queen Street East – Ministry of the Attorney General Court House was completed in 1922 in the Beaux Arts Classical style. It shows fine workmanship, good material and attention to details. The imposing, symmetrical, three-storey structure is built of orange-brown stone and brick. It is set back from the street on an elevated site and approached by a circular driveway. Its temple front facade consists of Ionic columns supporting a brick pediment.

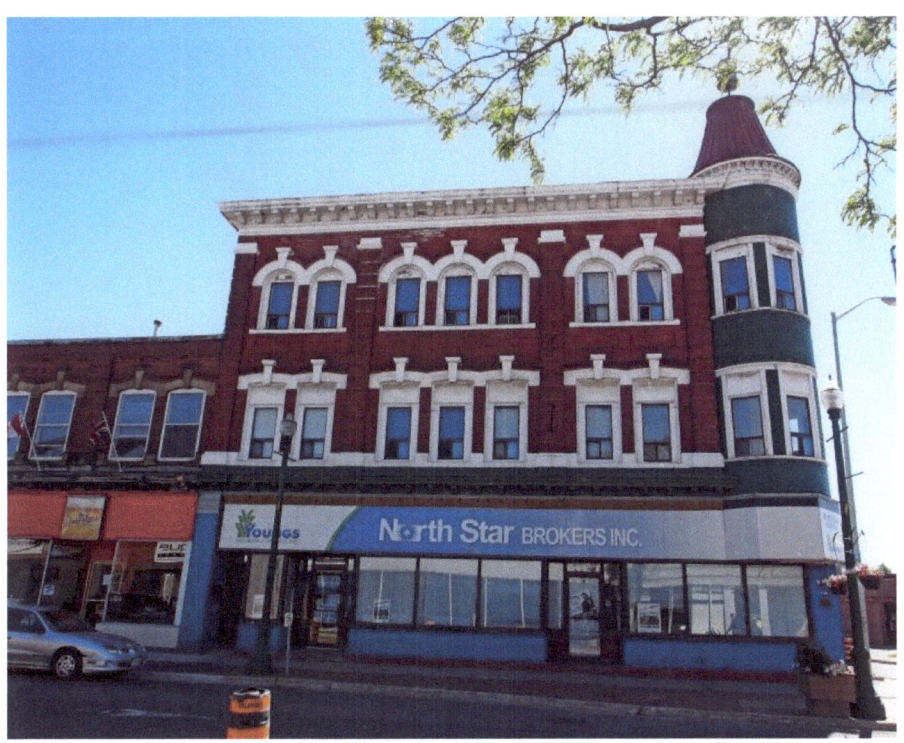

3-7 Queen Street East – Built at the turn of the century, the Barnes Block combines a Gothic corner turret with a late Victorian Italianate north façade. A mortar and pestle which rise from the truncated roof are a reminder that the building was originally built as a drug store.

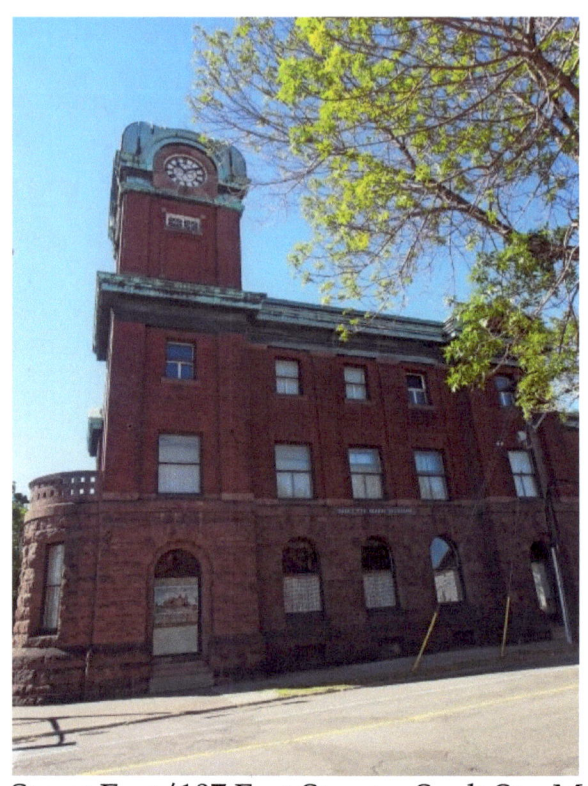

690 Queen Street East/107 East Street – Sault Ste. Marie Museum - The Old Post Office is an imposing three storey red brick and stone building featuring a clock tower. It is prominently located in downtown Sault Ste. Marie at the intersection of Queen Street East and East Street. Built between 1902 and 1906 as a federal building, it was purchased in 1982 by the City for use as the Sault Ste. Marie Museum. It is a fine example of turn of the century Federal architecture in Ontario, combining Victorian classicism with excellent workmanship. Exterior elements include classical pediments, pilasters and cornices, Romanesque stone arches with Italianate detailing and decorative features. Inside there is an oak staircase, an exquisite three-story light well and skylight, and a plated glass floor.

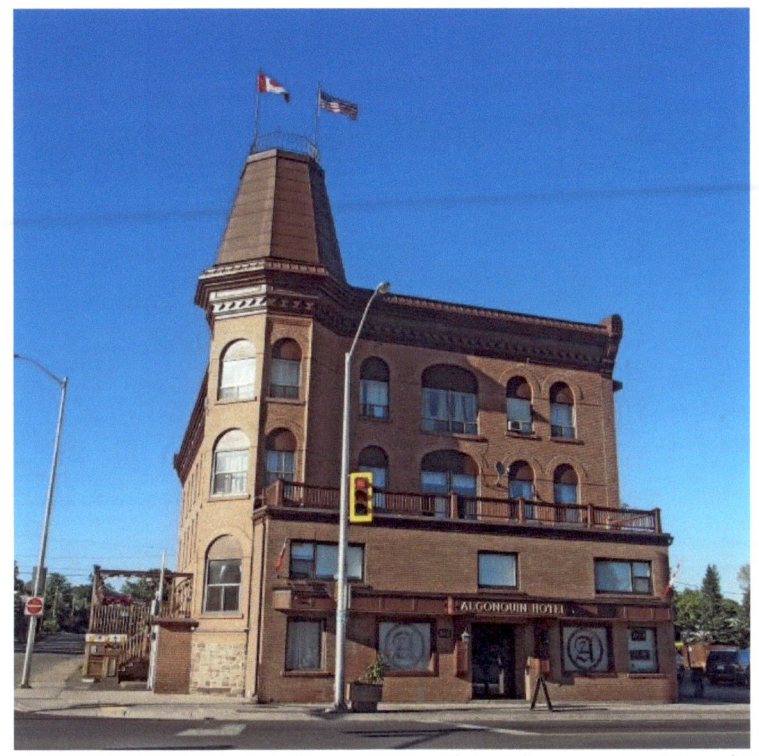

864 Queen Street East – Built in 1888, the Algonquin Hotel is a four-storey brick structure located in close proximity to the north shore of the St. Marys River on the northwest corner of Queen Street East and Pim Street. The Algonquin is the sole survivor of the large hotels built close to the turn of the twentieth century to cater to a rapidly expanding industrial center. These hotels were clustered around Sault Ste. Marie's docks to serve arriving settlers and workers. The hotel is a good example of Victorian commercial architecture. Key elements that reflect the architectural style are the use of brick masonry, including the masonry arches over the windows, the truncated tent roof which caps the southwest polygonal corner of the hotel, the painted metal cornice on the Queen Street and Pim Street facades, and the chevron molding on the Queen Street and Pim Street cornices.

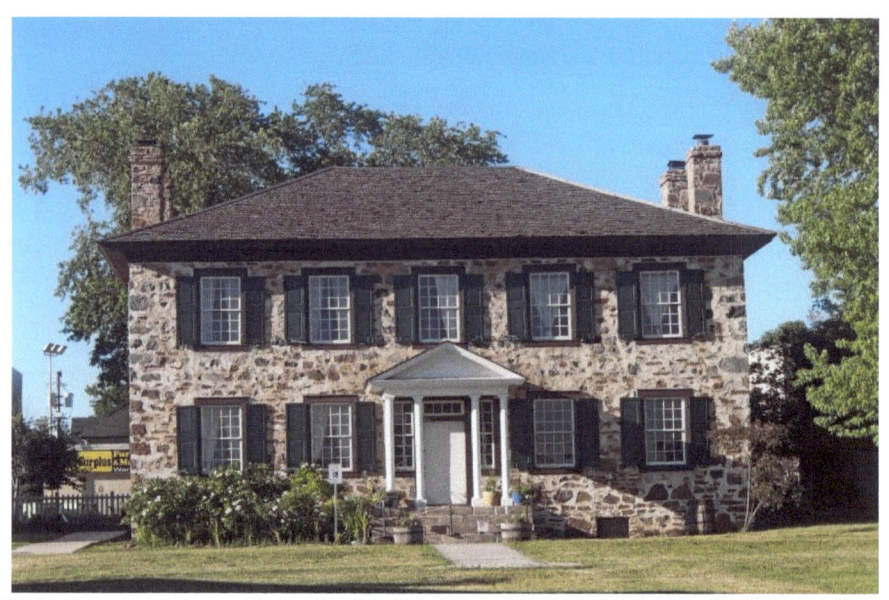

831 Queen Street East - The Ermatinger Old Stone House is a two-storey stone structure built on the north bank of the St. Mary's River near the rapids in Sault Ste. Marie. The house provides a link to Sault Ste. Marie's role in the fur trade and to one of its earliest settlers. Charles Oakes Ermatinger, a member of a prominent Montreal family who joined the Northwest Company and married Charlotte Katawabeda, the daughter of the Paramount Chief of the Ojibway, built the house in 1812-1814 of local red sandstone in a style characteristic of vernacular Georgian architecture but employed Quebec construction techniques. The house quickly became the center of government in the northwest part of the province and of the business and social life of the district. It later served as the first courthouse, a post office and a hotel. The house served as the headquarters of Sir Garnet Wolseley in 1870 when the expedition he commanded stopped at Sault Ste. Marie enroute to quell the Red River Rebellion and to establish Canadian sovereignty over Manitoba and the Northwest Territories.

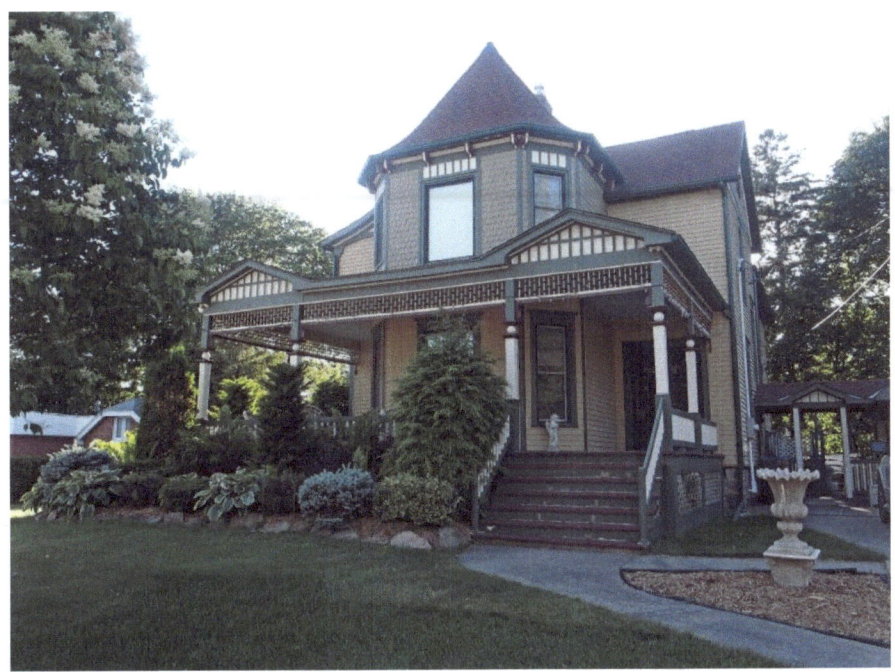

115 Upton Road - Built in 1902 as a family residence, the asymmetrical composition, turret and the variety and complexity of detail seen in the spindle work, porch supports and gable ends are typical of the Queen Anne style. It is a substantial, gracious and elegant framed dwelling on the west side of Upton Road in the east end of the older residential core. Edward L. Stewart, Manager of the International Lumber Company was the original owner and hired Thomas McKissock to begin construction in 1902. The plan is cruciform shaped with the head forming the main east elevation. The main facade and the wraparound veranda are the most prominent features of the house. The classical style veranda was originally accessed by two sets of identical steps at each end emphasized by a classical pediment. There are cornice brackets on the hexagonal turret below the cone-shaped roof.

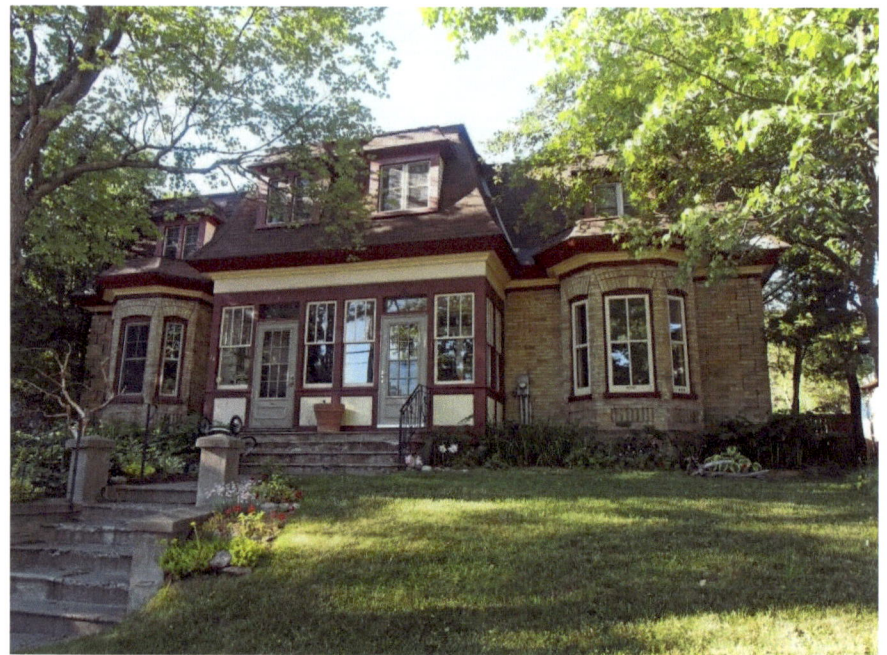

Built in 1889, 34-36 Herrick Street is a yellow brick residence located on a quiet dead-end street in the east end of the older residential core of Sault Ste. Marie. This house is an early example of Second Empire style architecture. The south elevation of the main house faces the street and was built in a symmetrical fashion. It is heightened by a projecting central frontispiece that continues up into a mansard roof which was originally sheathed with cedar shingles. Around the turn of the century, a demising wall was constructed through the middle of the house and the front porch was rebuilt to accommodate separate front entrances for two semi-detached units.

Lake Superior, Wawa, Dryden, Kenora, Ontario – My Top 8 Picks

Lake Superior is the largest freshwater lake in the world by surface area, and the third largest in volume. If the coast of Lake Superior was unraveled into a highway, it would extend 2,939 kilometers (1826 miles). The deepest spot is 406 meters (1,322 feet). Lake Superior presented many challenges to shipping. As interest in the resources of the north grew, investors wanted a more reliable form of transportation and the Algoma Central Railway was built. It was intended to bring iron ore and pulp logs from Wawa and Hearst to the mills of Sault Ste. Marie. With the completion of the railroad in 1914, loggers, tourists and artists travelled to places that had been difficult to reach.

Before Lake Superior Provincial Park was created, a group of artists came to paint pictures of Canada. J.E.H. Macdonald found a multi-channeled falls which he painted showing the foam, the reflections, the colors and the magic. These artists were experimenting with new techniques that showed the ruggedness and beauty of the land. Each fall between 1918 and 1922, members of the Group of Seven painted the newly accessible landscape of the Algoma region as the railway was built. They lived in a rented boxcar and travelled up and down the railway in a three-wheeled handcart called a velocipede. A canoe took them to locations away from the track. The bold new style of painting used vibrant colors.

The Agawa River Valley formed a natural pathway through the wilderness a section of the railway follows the route through the Agawa Canyon.

When the first Europeans travelled to the Wawa region in the late 1600s, they were introduced to a rugged landscape occupied by the Ojibway people. Wawa means clear water. Somewhere along the way wawa may have been mistranslated to wild goose instead of wewe which means snow goose. The wild goose story stuck and thus was born Wawa's legendary Wawa Goose.

Kenora is a small city situated on the Lake of the Woods in Northwestern Ontario, close to the Manitoba border. It is about two hundred kilometers (124 miles) east of Winnipeg. Kenora's future site was in the territory of the Ojibway when the first European, Jacques de Novon, sighted Lake of the Woods in 1688. Pierre La Verendrye established a French trading post, Fort St. Charles, to the south of present-day Kenora near the current Canada/United States border in 1732, and France maintained the post until 1763 when it lost the territory to the British in the Seven Years' War. In 1836 the Hudson's Bay Company established a post on Old Fort Island, and in 1861, the Company opened a post on the mainland at Kenora's current location.

In 1878, the company surveyed lots for the permanent settlement of *Rat Portage* ("portage to the country of the muskrat") — the community kept that name until 1905, when it was renamed Kenora.

Gold and the railroad were both important in the community's early history: gold was first discovered in the area in 1850, and by 1893, twenty mines were operating within 24 kilometers (15 miles) of the town. The first Canadian ocean-to-ocean train passed through in 1886 on the Canadian Pacific Railway.

A highway was built through Kenora in 1932, becoming part of Canada's first coast-to-coast highway in 1943, and then part of the Trans-Canada Highway. In 1967, the year of the Canadian Centennial, Kenora erected a sculpture known as Husky the Muskie. It has become the town's mascot and one of its most recognizable features.

A dramatic bank robbery took place in Kenora on May 10, 1973. An unknown man entered the Canadian Imperial Bank of Commerce heavily armed. After robbing the bank, the robber was preparing to enter a city vehicle driven by undercover police officer Don Milliard. A sniper positioned across the street shot the robber causing the explosives he was carrying to detonate and kill the robber. Most of the windows on the shops on the main street were shattered as a result of the blast.

The importance of the logging industry declined in the second part of the 20th century, and the last log boom was towed into Kenora in 1985. The tourist and recreation industries have become more important.

Dryden is the second-largest city in the Kenora District of North-western Ontario. It is located on Wabigoon Lake.

The Dryden area is part of the Ojibway nation, which covers a large area from Lake Huron in the east to Lake of the Woods and beyond. The Ojibway are nomadic with groups from family to village size moving over the land with the seasons and the availability of game or the necessities of life.

The settlement was founded as an agricultural community by John Dryden, Ontario's Minister of Agriculture in 1895. While his train was stopped at what was then known as Barclay Tank to re-water, he noticed clover growing and decided to found an experimental farm the following year. The farm's success brought settlers from other areas and the community came to be known as New Prospect.

Pulp and paper came to the town in 1910. Today, its main industries are agriculture, tourism and mining. The town was the site of the March 10, 1989 crash of Air Ontario Flight 1363 which killed twenty-four people.

Dryden is known by people passing by as the home of "Max the Moose", Dryden's 5.6 metres (18 foot) high mascot on the Trans-Canada Highway.

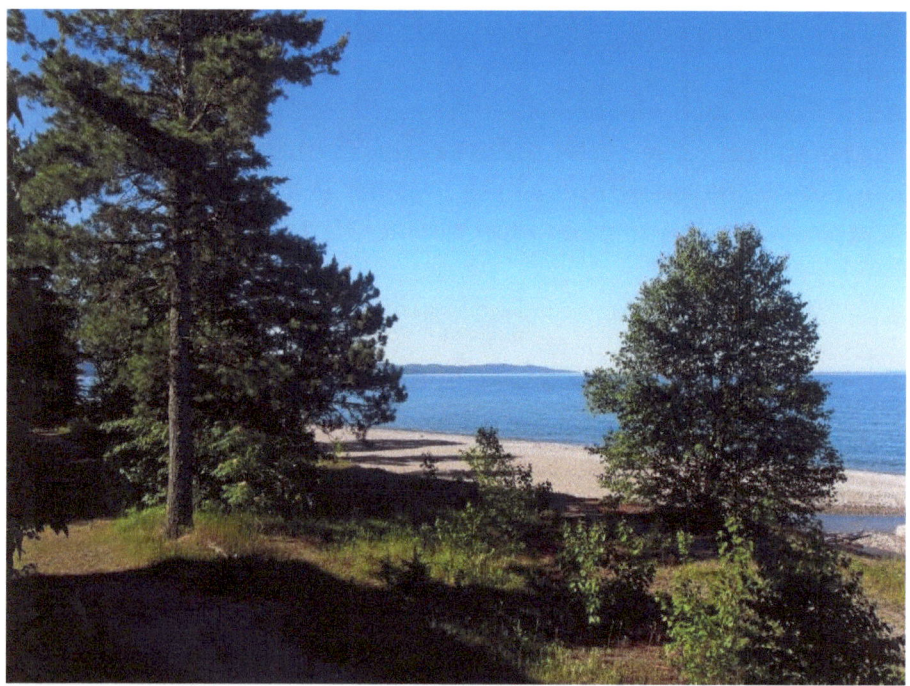

Lake Superior

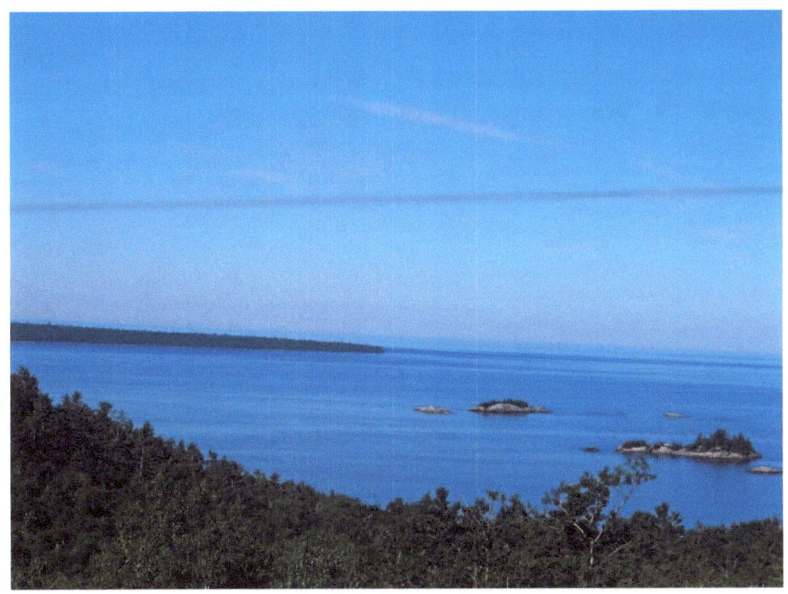

Lake Superior

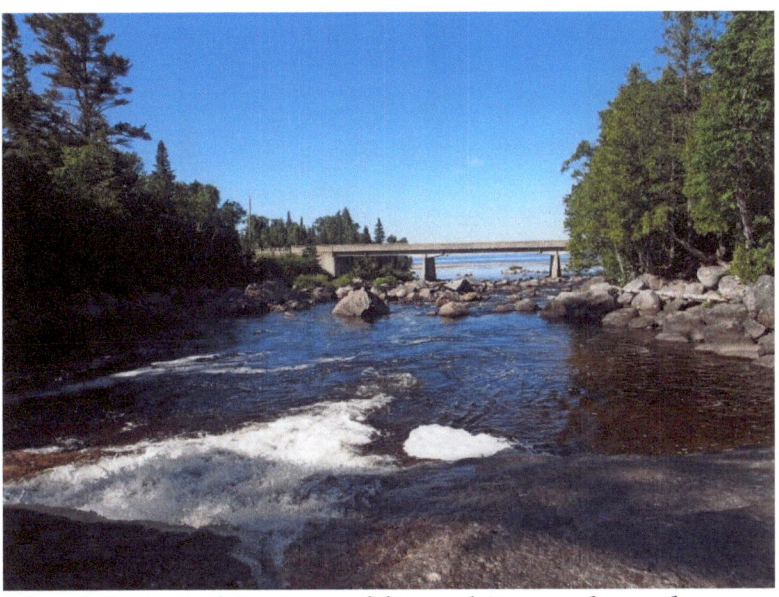

To the Ojibway, this river of fine white sand was known as Pinguisibi.

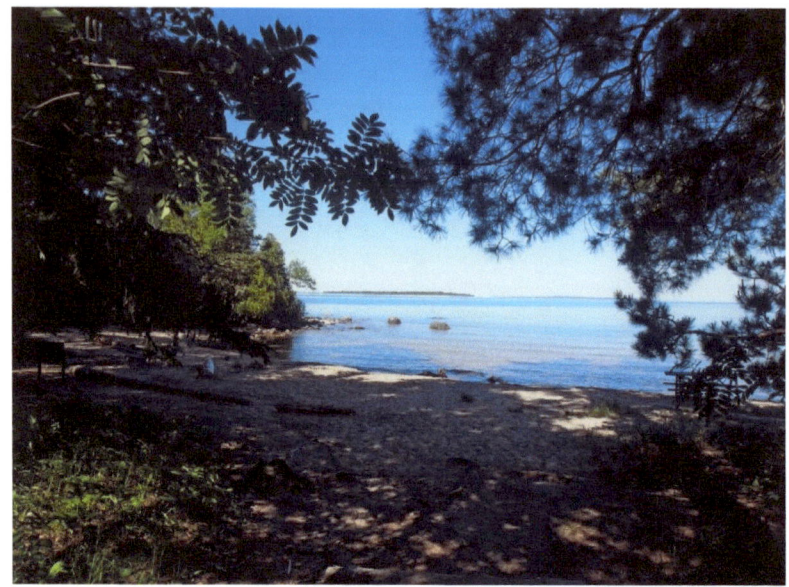

Here in the shelter of the Lizard Islands, the waters are warmer and shallower. The sand beaches of Katherine Cove are a great place for relaxing and having a picnic.

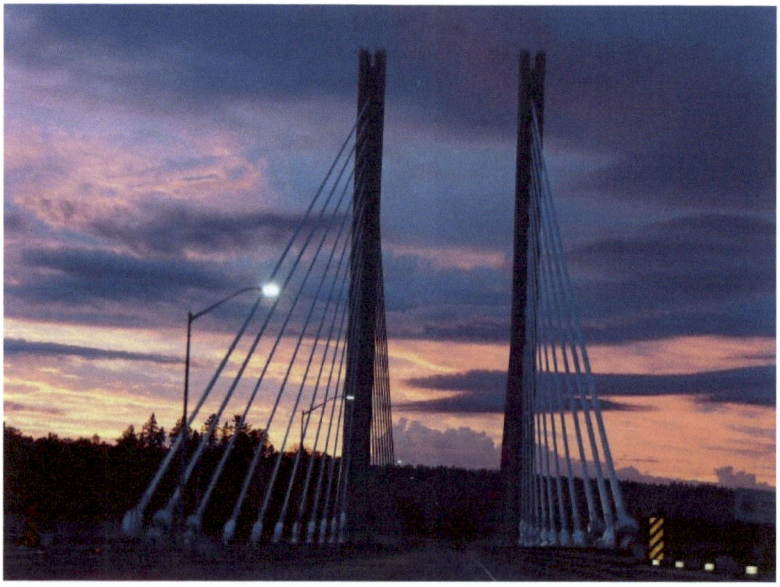

Nipigon Bridge at sunset

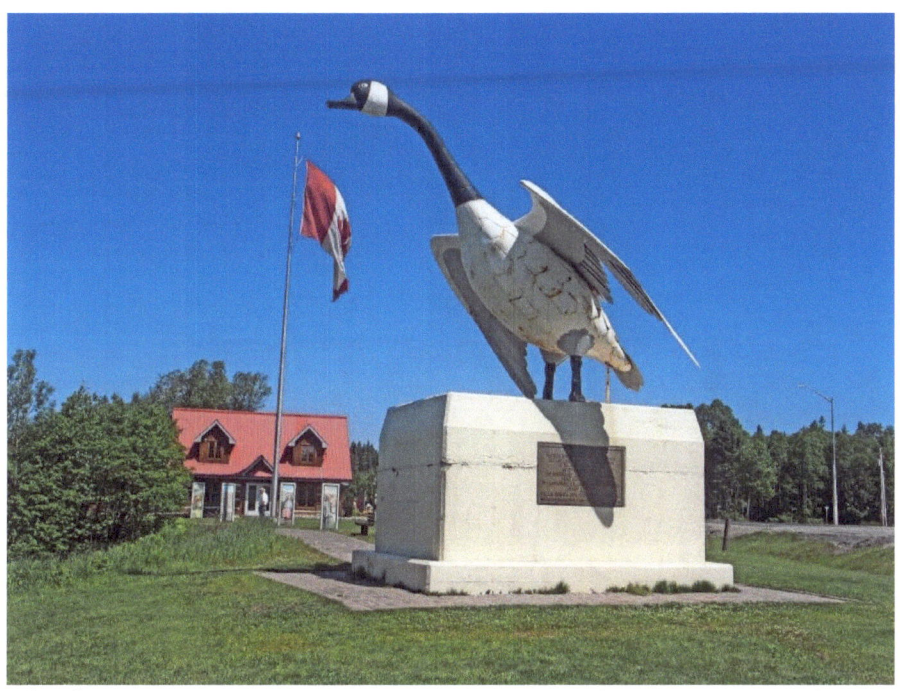

The famous Wawa Goose gazes out over the Trans-Canada Highway as it carries traffic through the Magpie River Valley. The Magpie River travels about one hundred and thirty kilometers over a number of scenic waterfalls (Steephill Falls, Magpie High Falls, and Silver Falls) until it merges with the Michipicoten River half a kilometer from its mouth on Lake Superior.

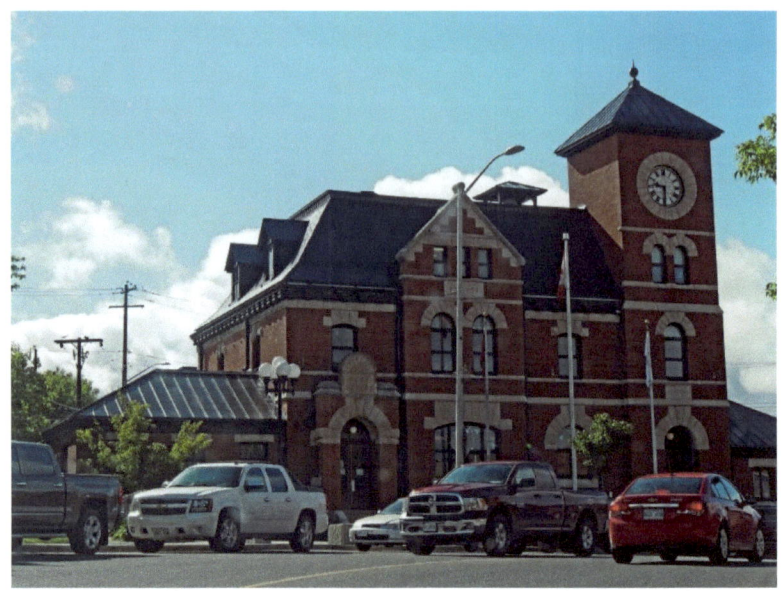

Kenora Post Office – A.D. 1898 – Second Empire style – mansard roof with dormers, dichromatic brickwork, banding, three-storey clock tower

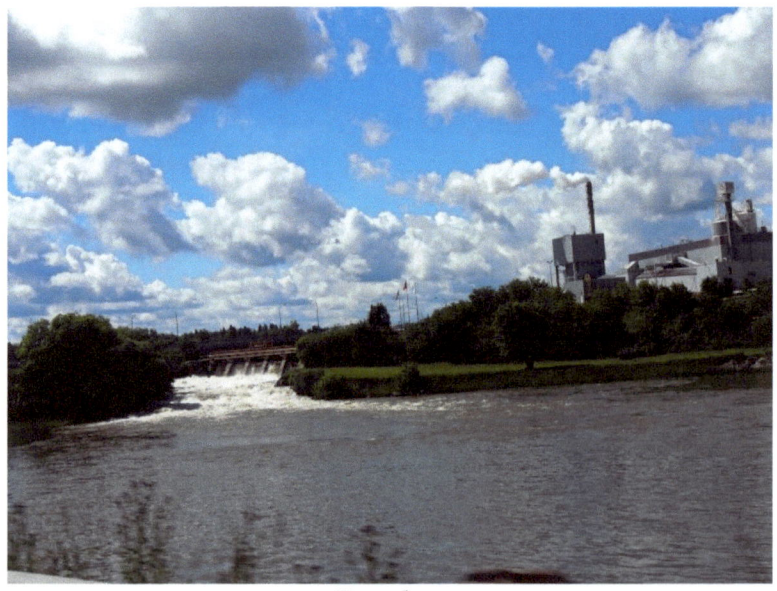

Dryden

Thunder Bay, Ontario – Part 1 – Port Arthur - My Top 12 Picks

The City of Thunder Bay has three histories. The twin cities of Fort William and Port Arthur were amalgamated in 1970. Thunder Bay's past is linked with the parallel but separate pasts of the two cities.

Port Arthur was a city in Northern Ontario which amalgamated with Fort William and the townships of Neebing and McIntyre to form the city of Thunder Bay in January 1970.

With Confederation in 1867, Simon James Dawson was employed to construct a road and route from Thunder Bay on Lake Superior to the Red River Colony. The depot on the lake, where supplies were landed and stored acquired its first name in May 1870. It was named Prince Arthur's Landing in honour of Prince Arthur, son of Queen Victoria who was serving with his regiment in Montreal.

Prospering from the CPR railway construction boom of 1882–1885, Port Arthur was incorporated as a town in March 1884, one year after acquiring its new name. The CPR erected Thunder Bay's and western Canada's first terminal grain elevator on the bay in 1883. The end of CPR construction along the north shore of Lake Superior and the CPR's decision to centralize its operations along the lower Kaministiquia River brought an end to Port Arthur's prosperity. Silver mining had been the mainstay of the economy for most of the 1870s.

The silver mining boom of the 1880s came to an end with the passage by the U.S. Congress of the McKinley Tariff in October 1890. The town was in dire economic straits until 1897–1899 when the entrepreneurs William Mackenzie and Donald Mann acquired the Ontario and Rainy River Railway and the Port Arthur, Duluth and Western Railway, and chose Port Arthur as the Lake Superior headquarters for the Canadian Northern Railway. Port Arthur thrived as a trans-shipment and grain handling port for the CNR after the railway line was opened to Winnipeg in December 1901.

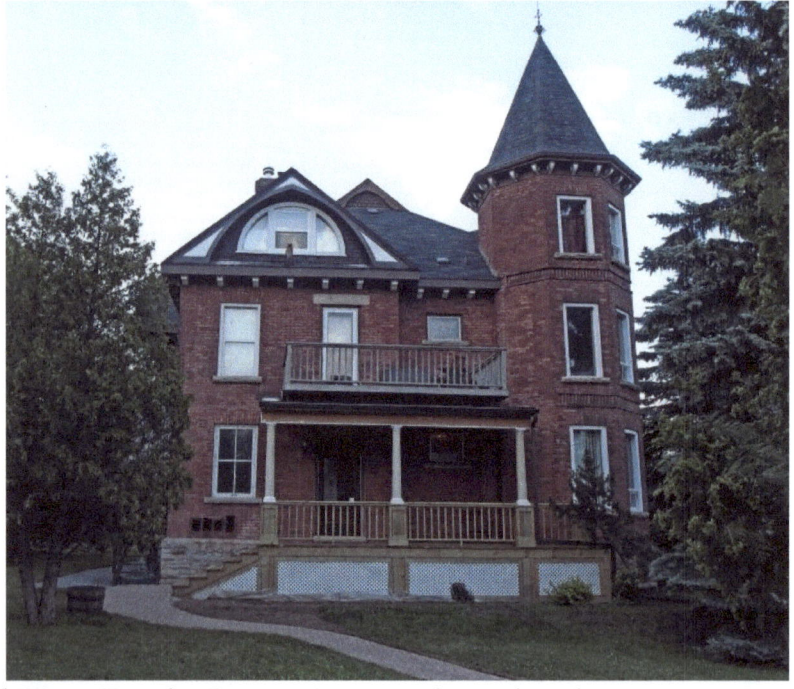

Red River Road - Queen Anne style with a three-storey tower with string courses between the windows; there are cornice brackets below the octagonal roof, and along the rest of the roofline; there is a second-floor balcony above the veranda. – Book 1

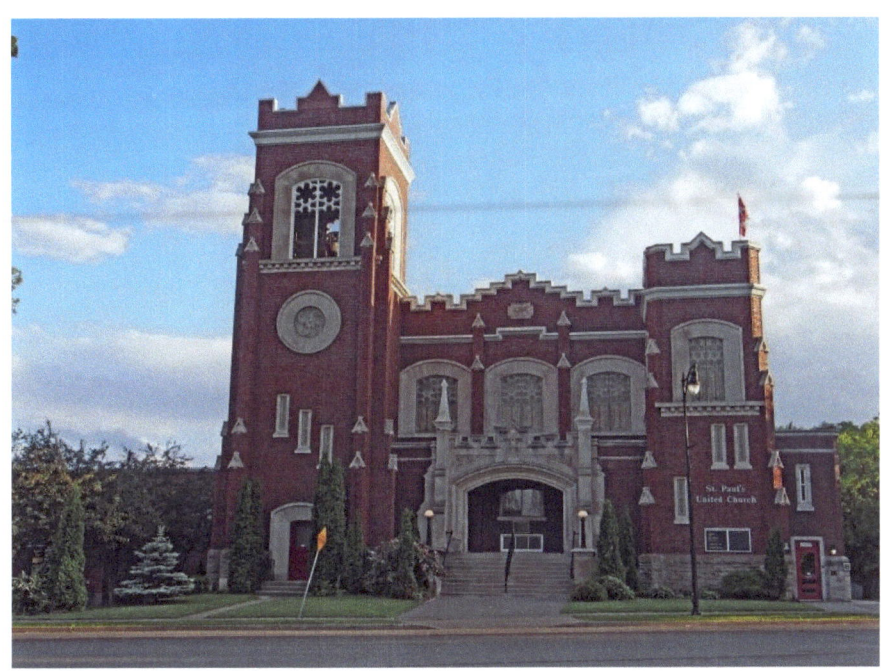

349 Waverley Street – St. Paul's United Church was built in 1914 in mixed styles of Georgian (stone window surrounds) and Late Gothic Revival (double towers, buttresses, and geometrical tracery). The façade appears complicated because of the two different towers, the arched entrance portico with balcony above, the elaborate tracery, and the crenellations on the rooflines. Constructed of local red brick, white Bedford limestone is used for accent. A wide segmental arch with moulding frames the covered entry; the doors are placed to the right and left, in the base of the towers. Above the arch there are spandrels filled with floral relief ornament. The piers to either side of the arch conclude with tall pointed finials. The north wall above the balcony has three large segmental arched windows with stone surrounds. Shallow stepped buttresses in brick with triangular capstones separate the windows. The honeycomb window tracery is applied to the windows rather than the structure. A date stone, 1913, is located above the window. – Book 1

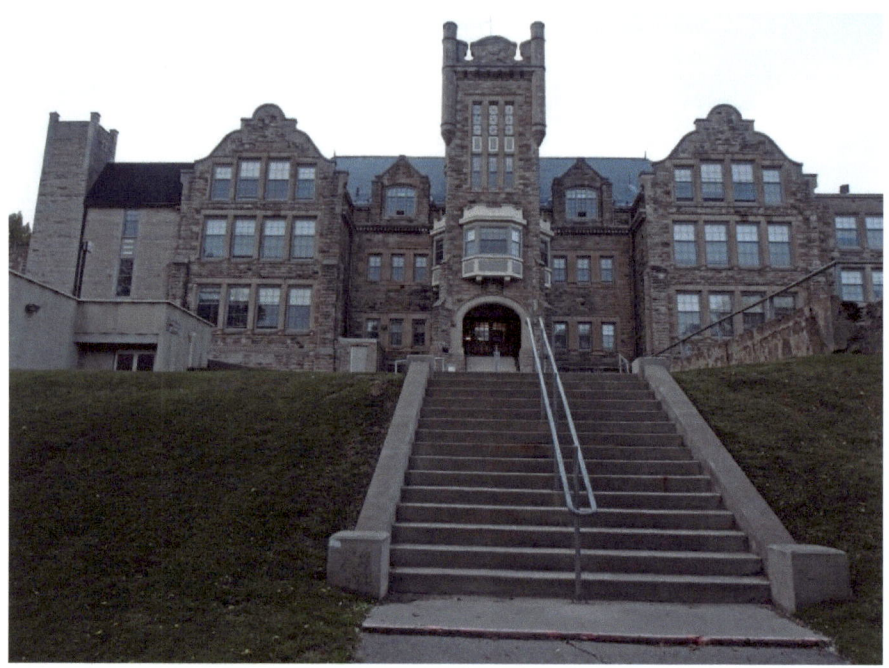

401 Red River Road – Port Arthur Collegiate Institute was constructed in 1909 of Simpson Island stone in the Queen Anne style. Due to decreasing enrollment, the school was closed in 2007. Lakehead University purchased the building and it is now the Bora Laskin Faculty of Law. Originally symmetrical, the school has a four-storey central tower flanked by two three-storey wings. The curved step-gables of the wings repeat the curved crenellations atop the tower. Rounded battlements project from the topmost corners of the tower and oriel windows from the second level. The entrance is on the first floor of the tower and reached through a round arch. Both the tower and the wings have buttresses at the corners. – Book 1

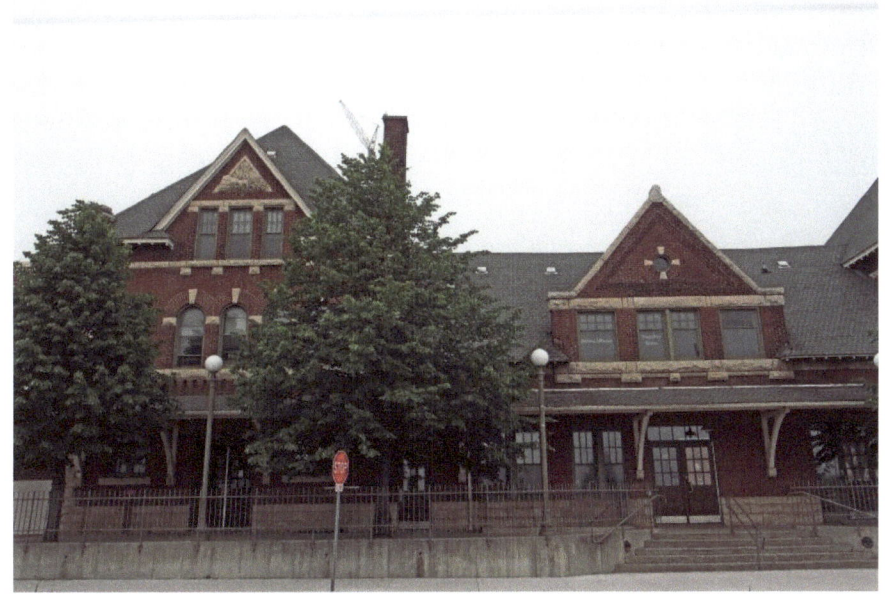

9 Water Street North – The Canadian National Railway Station was constructed in 1906 in the Chateauesque style. Brick is used on a symmetrical plan with Tyndall limestone used in the foundation and for decorative elements. The solid symmetrical arrangement of the masses and windows, combined with the Scottish Baronial style (the most noticeable characteristic of which is the bartizan, an overhanging corner turret), very high pitched roofs, multiple dormer windows, and crenellated turrets qualify this building as being a prime example of the "Railroad Gothic style" developed by the railway companies at the beginning of the twentieth century and is uniquely Canadian.

The plan of this brick building with pitch-faced limestone trim consists of a long, low, gabled central section. The large square end towers have centrally hipped roofs. The towers each have a central gable with three square-headed windows under one lintel course, with a string course, supported by stone corbels, at the windowsill level. Above the windows there is a triangular tablet bearing a wheat sheaf, the letters CNR and the date 1905, in relief. The second storey contains a triplet of round-headed windows with stone imposts and keystones; at the windowsill level there is a string course supported by a brick corbel table. The second storey of the central section consists of a parapeted gable with a bull's eye window below it. There is a frame canopy over the first storey across the full length of the east wall; it is supported on frame brackets that rest on stone corbels. All the corners of the building have quoining. There is a tall brick chimney on the east slope of the roof over the central section. – Book 2

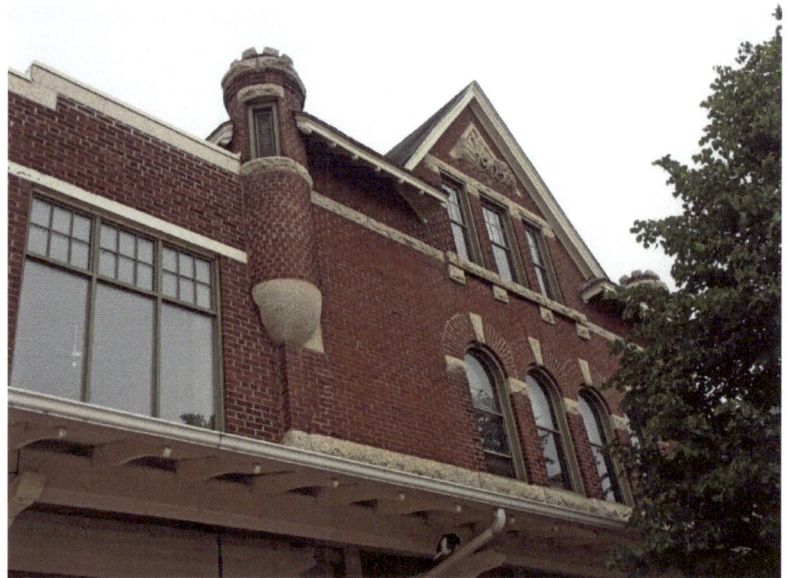

9 Water Street North end - The tower corners have bartizans with loophole windows, and stone bottoms and battlements.

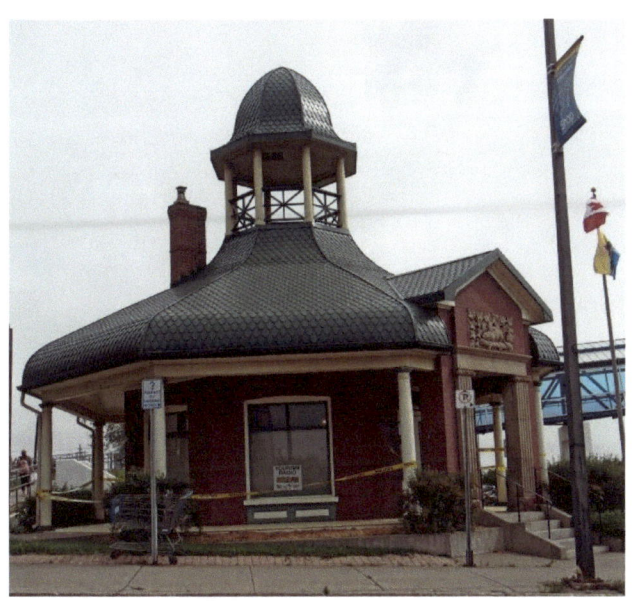

170 Red River Road – The Pagoda Visitor Centre was constructed in 1909. It was built specifically to capture the attention of visitors to Port Arthur. It is an eclectic mixture of Roman, Greek (the peristyle formed by the columns surrounding the outside of the building which support the roof and is characteristic of basic elements of western architecture), Indian Islamic (mushroom or umbrella-shaped roof) and Scandinavian architecture. The cupola on top of the roof was originally designed so that bands could play to welcome visitors. Above the entrance is a large carved stone panel with a beaver and maple leaves. – Book 2

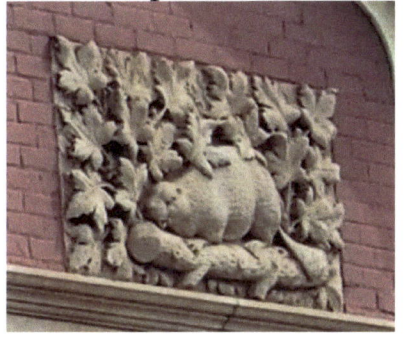

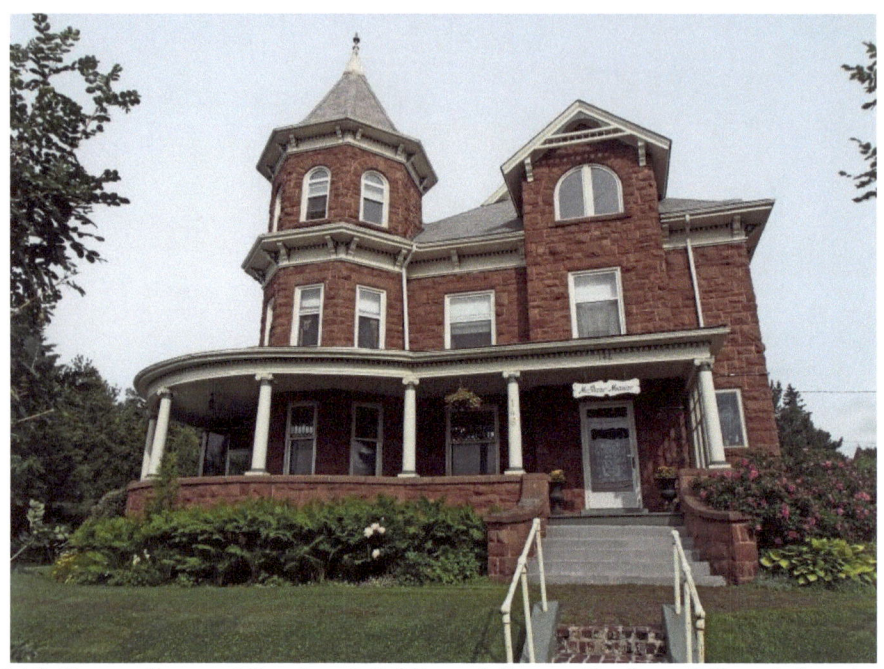

146 Court Street North – McVicar Manor Bed and Breakfast is a 1906 Edwardian red brick home with three spacious rooms. It has a three-storey turret, and a two-and-a-half tower-like bay, cornice brackets, Ionic pillars supporting a wraparound veranda. – Book 2

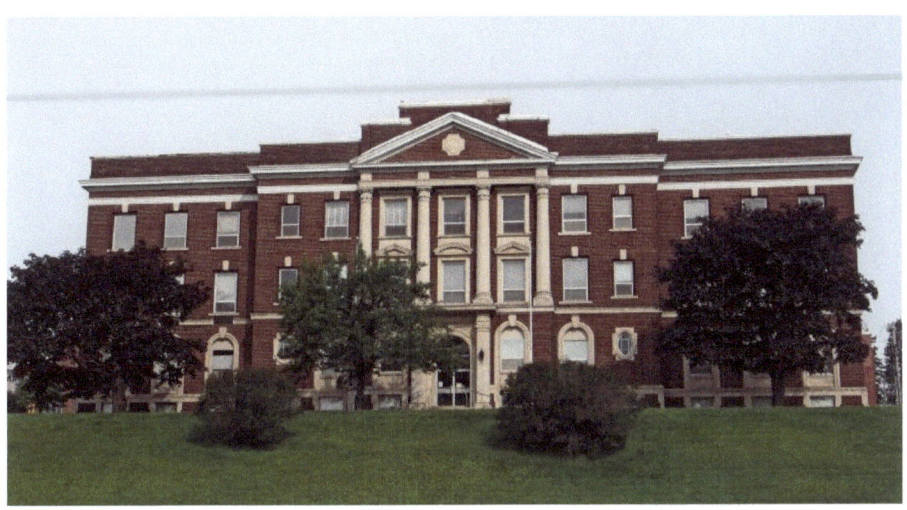

277 Camelot Street – The District Court House was constructed in 1924 in the Classical Revival style. The building is symmetrical and is constructed of structural steel with brick walls. The imposing exterior of the building includes the Classical pediment above the main entrance which is supported by four Corinthian columns. The white Tyndall limestone used for the columns, sills and the window casement rim contains visible fossils. – Book 2

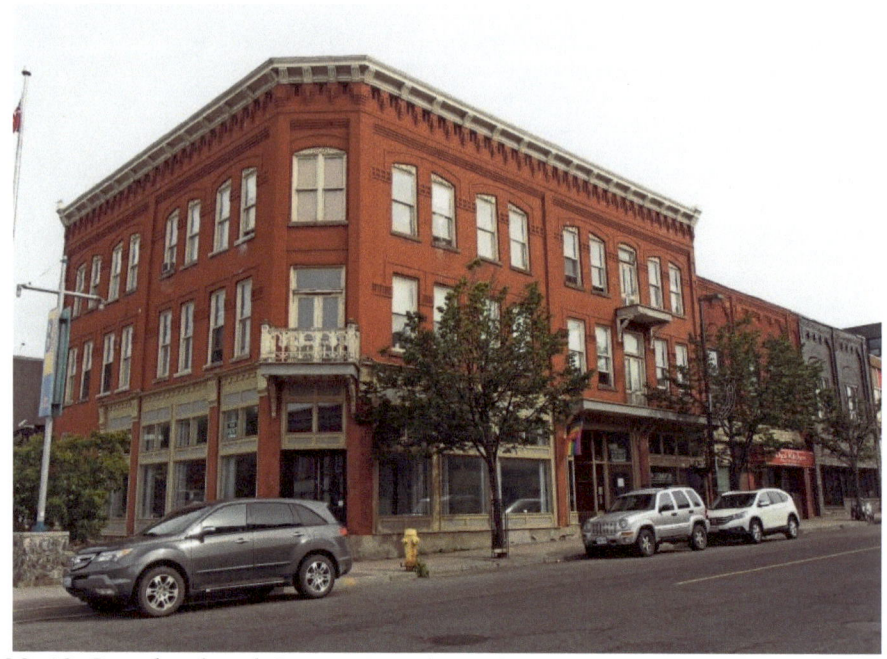

38-40 Cumberland Street South at the corner of Lincoln – The former Ottawa House hotel is a distinctive three-storey business block constructed of red brick in 1888. There is a wooden cornice at the roofline, decorative brick brackets which visually extend the cornice, and rectangular areas of patterned brickwork between the windows. Splayed brick forms an arch between the pairs of windows and the single window on the third-floor windows, and there are brick voussoirs above the second-storey windows. There is a second-floor balcony above the corner entrance. The hotel was advertised as having fifty rooms, baths, a steam furnace, and electric light. – Book 2

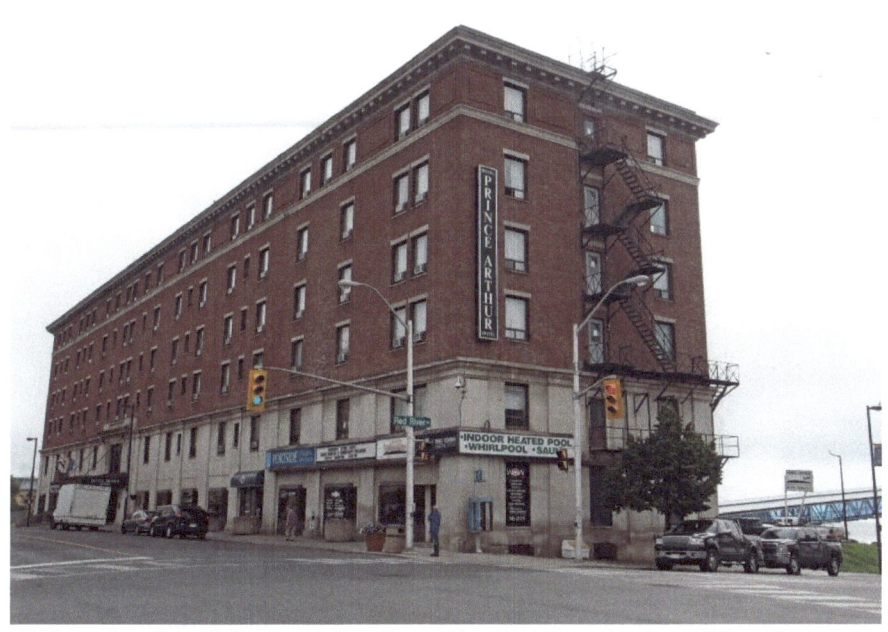

17 Cumberland Street North – The Prince Arthur Hotel was built in 1911. The rooms were well heated and lighted; each one had hot and cold running water. The cost of a room for the night was as low as one dollar. Most early visitors to the Lakehead arrived by steamship or by rail, and disembarked at the stations near the Prince Arthur. The hotel was constructed of brick and stone and had a marble staircase. Six stories high, the building has prominent lintels above all upper floor windows, impressive massing, and decorative brick work on the top storey. There are slightly projecting pilasters on the stone portion of the building and a cut stone string-course between the fifth and sixth storeys. The original lake side entrance had formal terraced gardens and lawns that cascaded down to the Canadian Pacific Railway Station. The hotel was expanded in 1912 and again in 1920. A dining room, barbershop, newsstand, washrooms, writing room, balcony and extra wings were added. – Book 2

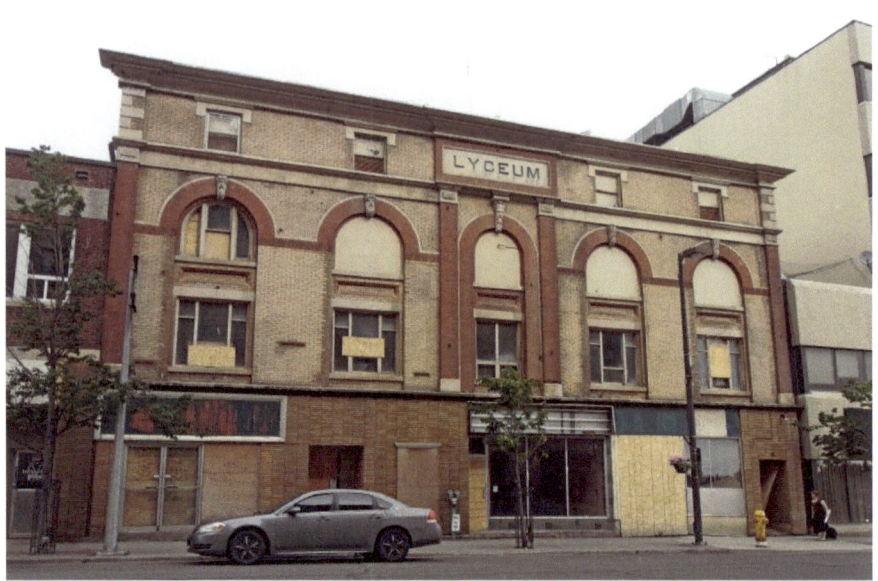

12-22 Cumberland Street North – The Lyceum Theatre was built in 1909 to accommodate travelling shows and then later it was a movie theatre; now it is several offices and stores. Some of the significant architectural features are keystones with bearded faces, segmented semi-circular windows, and a large stone panel in the center of the façade with the name LYCEUM in large letters. The building is steel framed with brick facing and stone trim. – Book 2

Thunder Bay, Ontario – Part 2 – Fort William - My Top 19 Picks

Fort William was a city in Northern Ontario located on the Kaministiquia River at its entrance to Lake Superior. It amalgamated with Port Arthur and the townships of Neebing and McIntyre to form the city of Thunder Bay in January 1970. The city's Latin motto was *A posse ad esse* (From a Possibility to an Actuality) featured on its coat of arms designed in 1900 by town officials. "On one side of the shield stands an Indian dressed in the paint and feathers of the early days; on the other side is a French voyageur; the centre contains an elevator, a steamship and a locomotive, while the beaver surmounts the whole."

In about 1684, Daniel Greysolon, Sieur du Lhut, established a trading post near the mouth of the Kaministiquia River. French authorities closed this post in 1696 because of a glut on the fur market. In 1717, a new post, Fort Kaministiquia, was established at the river mouth. The post was abandoned in 1758 or 1760 during the British conquest of New France.

In 1803, the Nor'Westers established a new fur trading post on the Kaministiquia River and the post was named Fort William in 1807 after William McGillivray, chief director of the North West Company from 1804-1821. After the union of the North West Company with the Hudson's Bay Company (HBC) in 1821 most trade shifted to York Factory on Hudson Bay. Two townships (Neebing and Paipoonge) and the Fort William Town Plot were surveyed in 1859-60 and opened to settlement.

By 1883-84, the Montreal-based CPR syndicate, in collaboration with the Hudson's Bay Company, clearly preferred the low-lying lands along the lower Kaministiquia River to the exposed shores of Port Arthur, which required an expensive breakwater if shipping and port facilities were to be protected from the waves. The CPR subsequently consolidated all its operations there, erecting rail yards, coal-handling facilities, grain elevators and a machine shop.

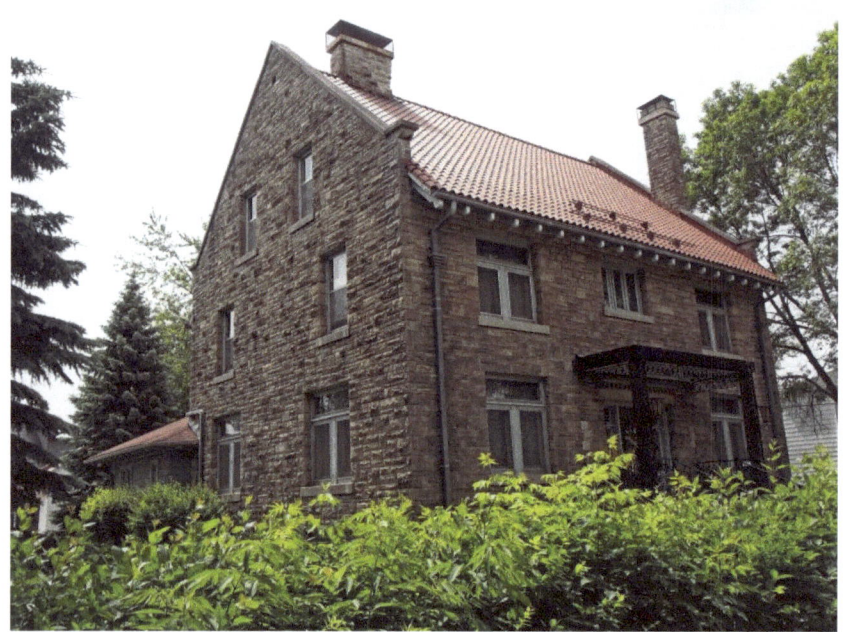

1306 Ridgeway Street East – It was constructed in 1911 with Simpson Island stone. This two and a half storey European style home has many unique architectural characteristics which include the prominent red tiling on the high-pitched gable roof as well as the light gray squared rubble that was used in the construction. The iron porch was added after Bishop E. Q. Jennings purchased the house in 1958. - Thunder Bay Book 3

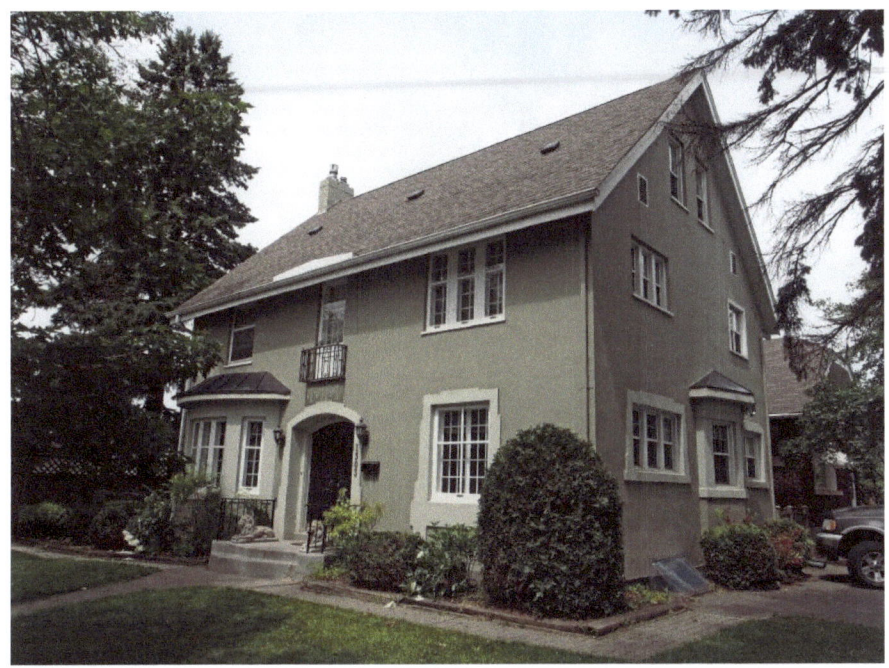

1303 Ridgeway Street East – Strachan Residence – Cecil R. Strachan, a local jeweler, was the first owner. It is built in a Revival Period style, has a stucco exterior in a light gray-green colour contrasted with hood moulds found around the main entrance and windows on the first storey. The entrance is embrasure with plain moulding. Above the entry is a window with a baluster barrier. The bay windows of the façade of the house are divided with glazing bars. - Thunder Bay Book 3

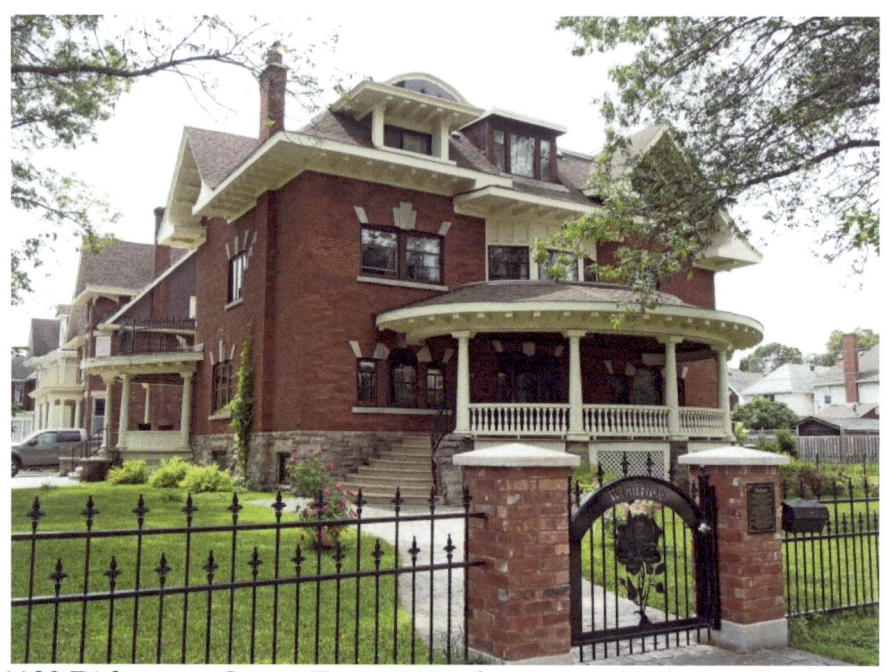

1100 Ridgeway Street East – Windrose was built in 1910 for Frederick and Cora Morris – he was a solicitor in Fort William beginning in 1897. Queen Anne Revival style – red brick contrasted with cut stone, wood and a rubble stone coursed foundation. The front façade is asymmetrical and the roofline is irregular. The central bay is flat topped, another bay has a rounded dormer, and the third bay has a pointed dormer. The façade has two Palladian windows on the first floor, and a second-floor bay window which suit the Queen Anne style. The house has two rounded verandas supported by classically inspired columns. - Thunder Bay Book 3

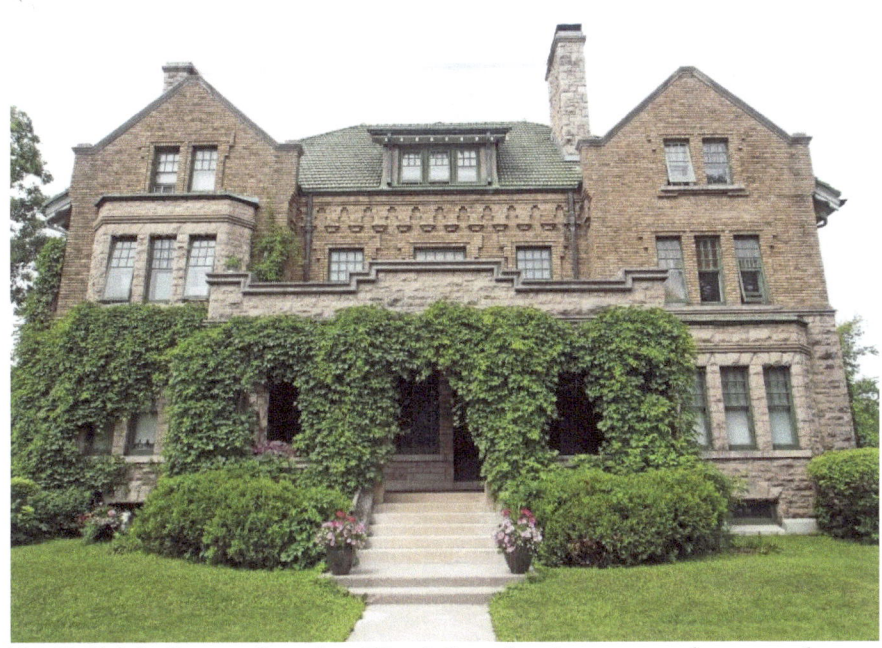

431 Selkirk Street South - The Murphy house and grounds, span a whole city block. They are a reminder of the days of Edwardian commercial wealth. The house is a three and a half storey home in brick and stone. James Murphy arrived in Fort William in 1884 and earned his fortune by establishing the James Murphy Coal Company, after having gained valuable experience as a fuel contractor for the Canadian Pacific Railway. The company shipped fuel throughout Northwestern Ontario and into Manitoba. Members of the Murphy family remained in the mansion after the death of James Murphy in 1928, and the subdivision of the house into apartments in 1946. - Thunder Bay Book 3

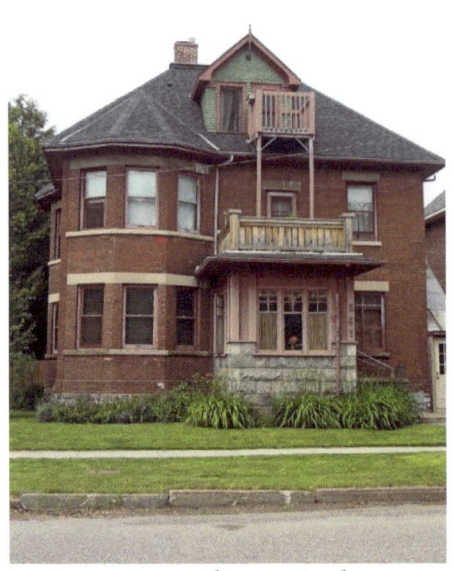

541 Norah Street – two-storey bay window, second and third floor balconies - Thunder Bay Book 3

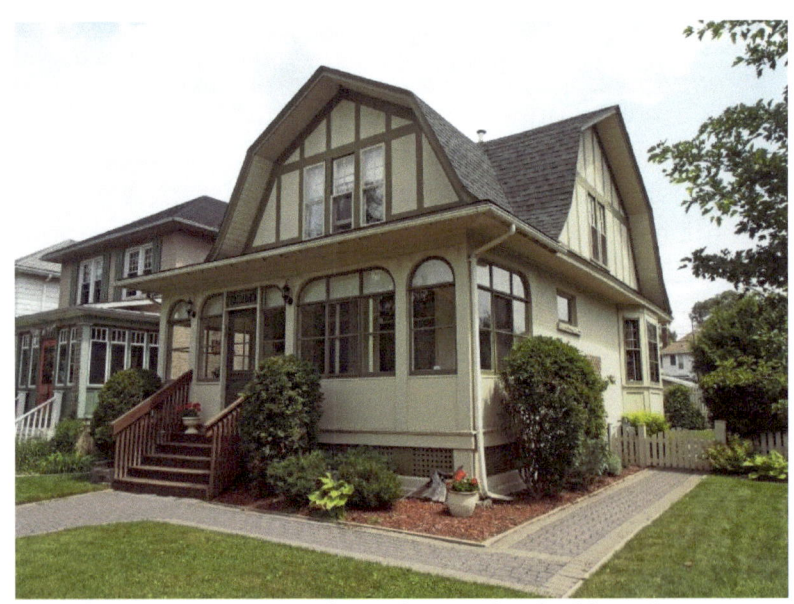

410 Norah Street – Neo-colonial – Tudor half-timbering on gables - Thunder Bay Book 3

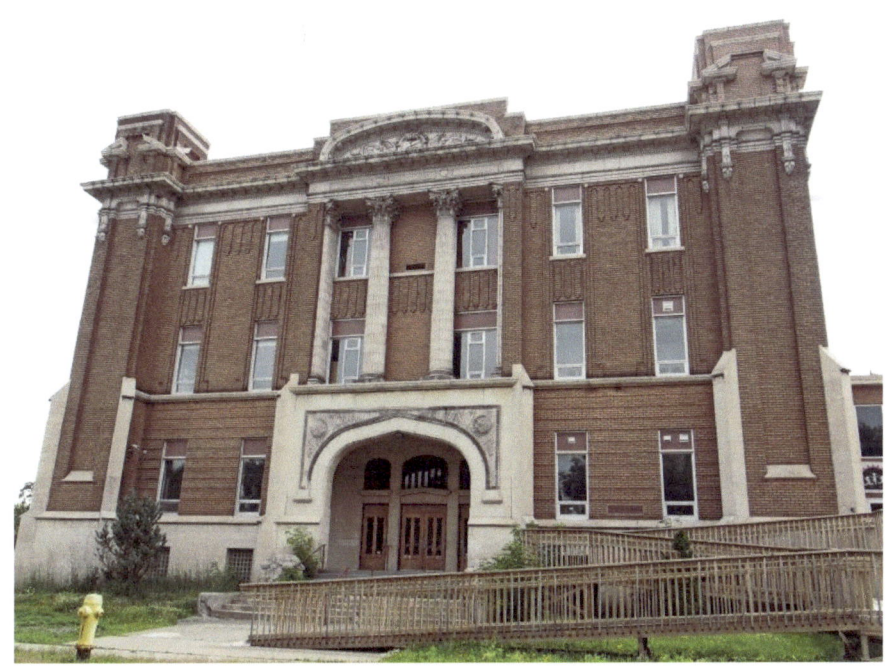

512 Marks Street South – Fort William Collegiate Institute was constructed in 1907 to house the ever increasing need for a secondary school in Fort William. A big reconstruction in 1918 added the Vocational Wing. A second addition was constructed in 1925, and a third in 1970. The stately structure acted as a symbol of social importance to the community. Constructed of brick and stone, the building is three and a half storeys high and is eclectic in design. The main façade, which faces Marks Street South repeats its main architectural features on both the Isabella and Catherine Street sides. The building boasts impressive stonework and features large columns with Corinthian capitals which span from the second to third storey. They are topped by a circular pediment with a decorated typanum below a stepped parapet. The oak doors of the main entrance as well as the woodwork in the lobby area add to the stately décor of the structure. - Thunder Bay Book 3

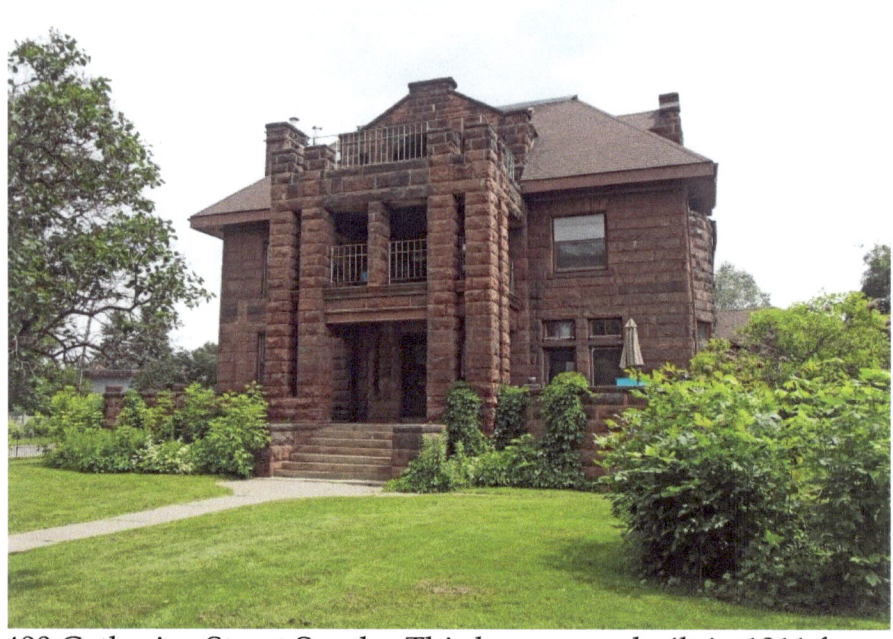

400 Catherine Street South - This house was built in 1911 for William Ross and his family. Ross worked as an engineer on the Canadian Pacific Railway and as the treasurer of Northern Engineering. Starting in 1947 the house was used by the Lakehead Board of Education. In 1966 it was sold and was divided into apartments and remains as such today. This two and a half storey Tudor Revival home was constructed of red sandstone. Architectural features include the massive three storey portico on the façade, and the truncated hipped roof. The north and south slopes of the roof each have a chimney. - Thunder Bay Book 3

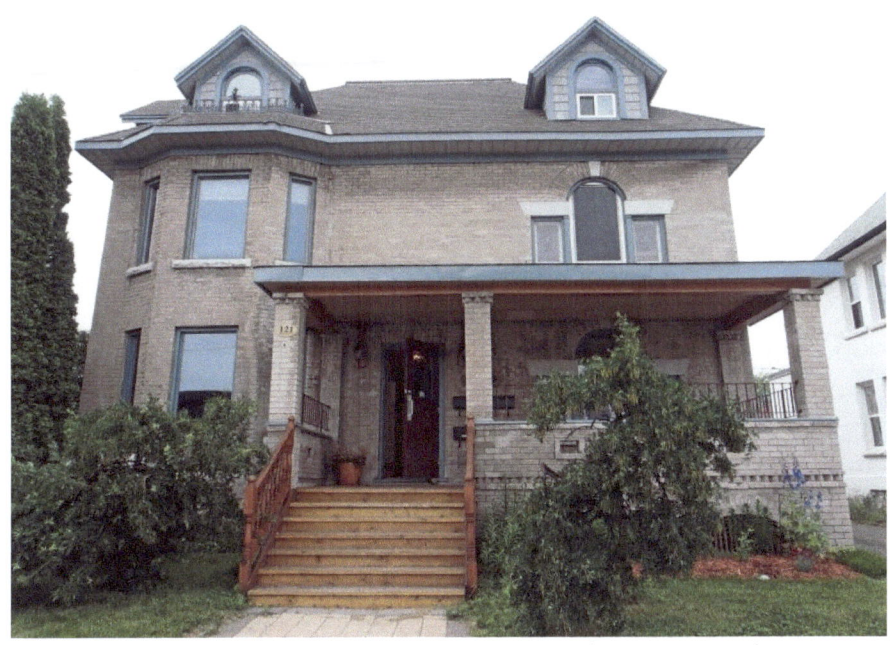

121 McKellar Street South - Built in 1907 for owner Thomas P. Kelley, a local merchant, the house was later sold to Dr. R. Kerr Dewar who had fought in the First World War, returned home to study medicine and purchased this home in 1920. The first floor was converted to a medical clinic in 1928. The building is a good example of Edwardian Classicism. It has metal cresting on one of the dormer windows. The first and second floors both have distinctive Palladian windows with prominent keystones. On the front façade, the centrally placed wood covered porch is supported by brick piers. There is a two-storey bay window. - Thunder Bay Book 4

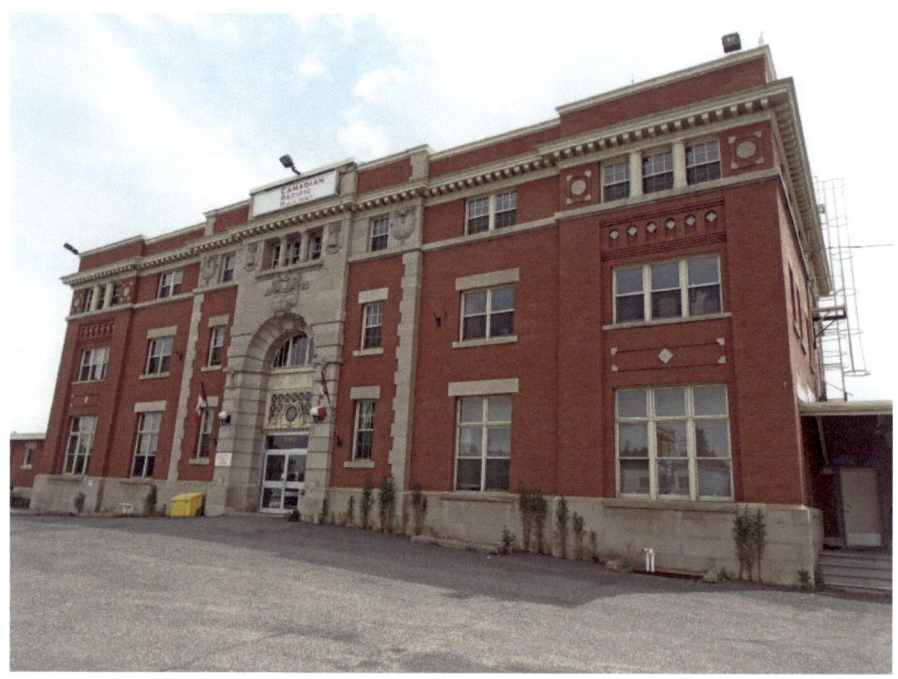

440 South Syndicate Avenue - Built in 1911 as a union station by the Canadian Pacific Railway (CPR) and the Grand Trunk Pacific Railway (GTPR), the station served as a passenger terminal and as administrative headquarters for the vast grain-handling facilities that were the foundation of the community. Union Station is a good example of Beaux-Arts design applied to a railway station. Notable architectural features include a projecting central bay with stone quoins and two wheat sheaves carved in Bedford stone, an arched entrance with a transom light, and projecting end bays with pilasters topped with decorative elements. - Thunder Bay Book 4

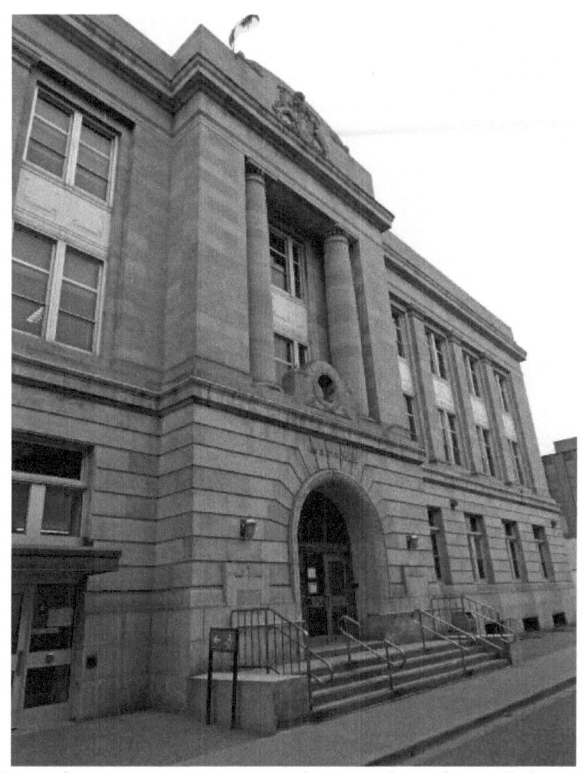

130 South Syndicate Avenue - The Federal Building represents a turning point in the development of Fort William. The Federal Building was constructed between 1934 and 1936. It is an example of the Beaux-Arts style that employs classical decorative elements to achieve a monumental effect. The building shows attention to symmetry, proportion and detail throughout. Excellent craftsmanship and materials are seen in the rich detailing of the exterior stonework and also in the opulence of the interior finishes. - Thunder Bay Book 4

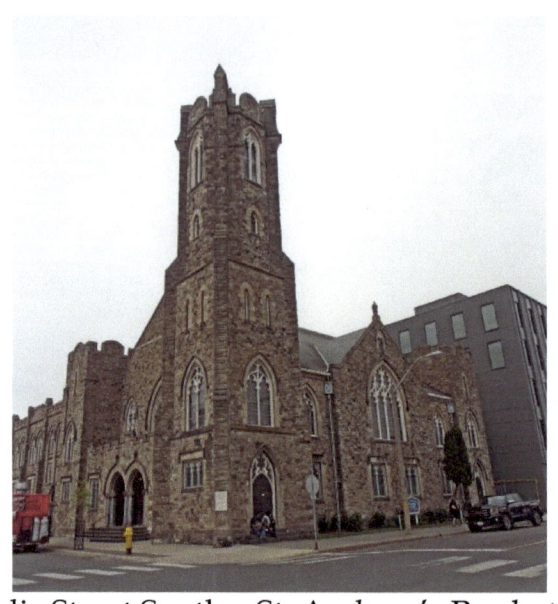

207-211 Brodie Street South – St. Andrew's Presbyterian Church was designed in the style of fourteenth century English Gothic. There is a massive tower at the northeast corner made from Simpson islet grey/white sandstone. The main entrance, which faces Brodie Street, has two Gothic arches with elaborate moulds and is supported at the center and on either side by ten massive, polished granite columns. The ornamental cap of Bedford stone is beautifully carved, the design at the center being the Maple Leaf, while the one on the right is carved into a Rose and on the left, the Scottish Thistle. The label mold around the arches is carved with Shamrocks; on the right arch is carved the Leek, representing Wales and on the left are the Lilies of France. These carvings are symbolic of the fact that everyone is welcome to the church. The main tower rises to a height of ninety-five feet and is supported by four angle buttresses. Square to the clock loft, it changes into an octagon and terminates in the well-known typical Gothic weathering of this period of architecture. - Thunder Bay Book 4

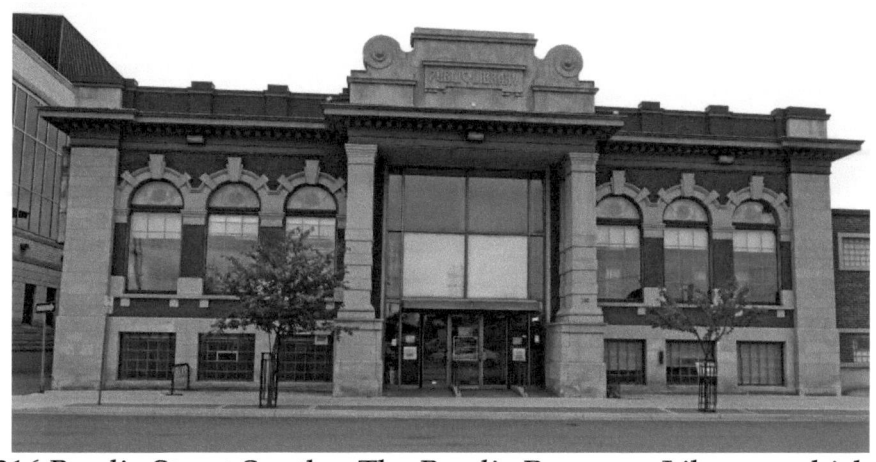

216 Brodie Street South – The Brodie Resource Library, which opened in 1912, followed the architectural guidelines established by its benefactor, Mr. Andrew Carnegie. Resembling Palladian Renaissance architecture, the library's symmetrical staircase entrance was embellished with a pair of Ionic columns enclosed by pilasters. Carnegie approached library design with symbolism in mind, and the staircase entrance was supposed to have denoted a person's rise through intellectual learning. Brodie Street Resource Library's entrance was renovated in 1966 to permit accessibility, and the pilasters were changed into square piers. The overall composition of the exterior is Neo-Renaissance in character. Red brick and limestone pilasters and columns rest on a heavy stone base. Arches and columns arranged symmetrically about the main entrance support a bracketed cornice. The cornice in turn supports a brick parapet which corresponds to the Renaissance balustrade. Other notable architectural features of the library are the arched windows and their surrounding decorative stonework, the stained-glass windows depicting famous authors, from Dante to Ibsen, the parapet inscribed 'Public Library,' and the ornamental scrolls which adorn it. - Thunder Bay Book 4

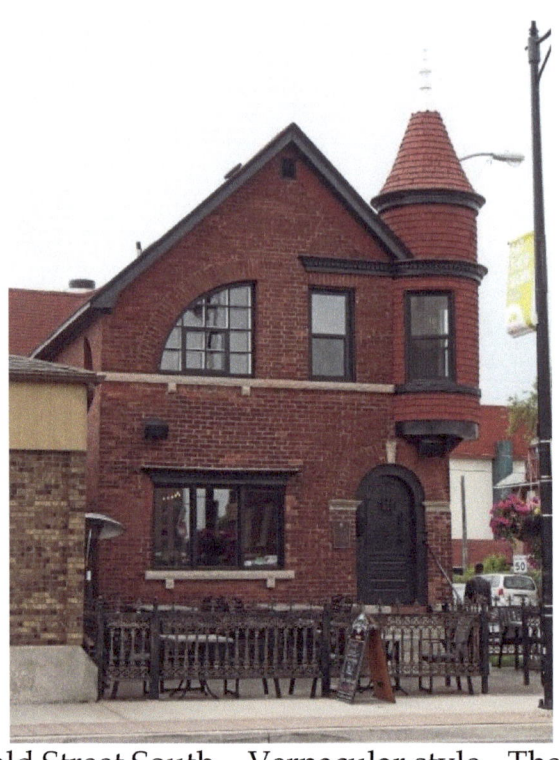

135 Archibald Street South – Vernacular style - The house which stands on the corner of Archibald and Miles Street was first owned by Sarah Jane and George Coo. It is thought that George designed the building which has an elegant and eclectic feel. The jutting turrets, arched entranceway and quarter-wheel windows are features which one wouldn't expect on such a modest-sized structure. The house is characterized by an ostentatious conical turret with faux brickwork façade. The windows are all of varied shapes and sizes, lending themselves to the overall eclecticism of the house. The large window on the main floor has a shelf entablature above it; there is also a large stone sill supported by brackets. Above the double-hung window on the second level is a molded shelf which begins rather abruptly and continues around the turret. - Thunder Bay Book 4

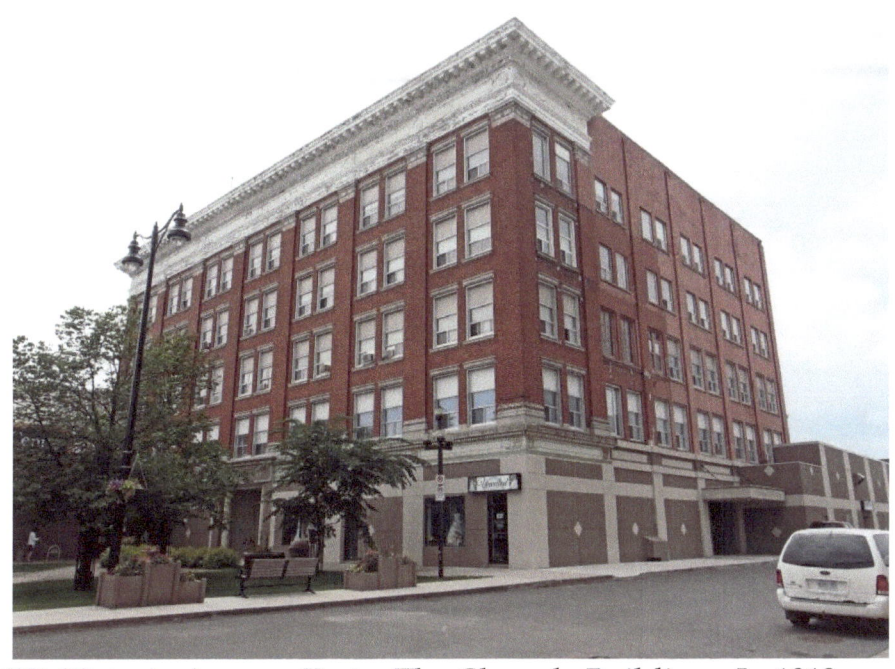

701 Victoria Avenue East – The Chapple Building - In 1913, Fort William was designated the headquarters of the Grain Commission. A prominent building was constructed in the community with the facilities to handle and inspect grain. The structure housed offices on the third floor and the bottom two storeys were rented to the Chapples Company as a department store. Chapples sold everything from "lady-ready-to-wear" to "hardware" and upon its opening in this building boasted a staff of one hundred. The façade of the building features Classical detailing. Some of the architectural features are large scale dentils located on the metal projecting cornice and brick piers with stone relief capitals creating seven bays. The building has a recessed entrance with Doric columns. - Thunder Bay Book 4

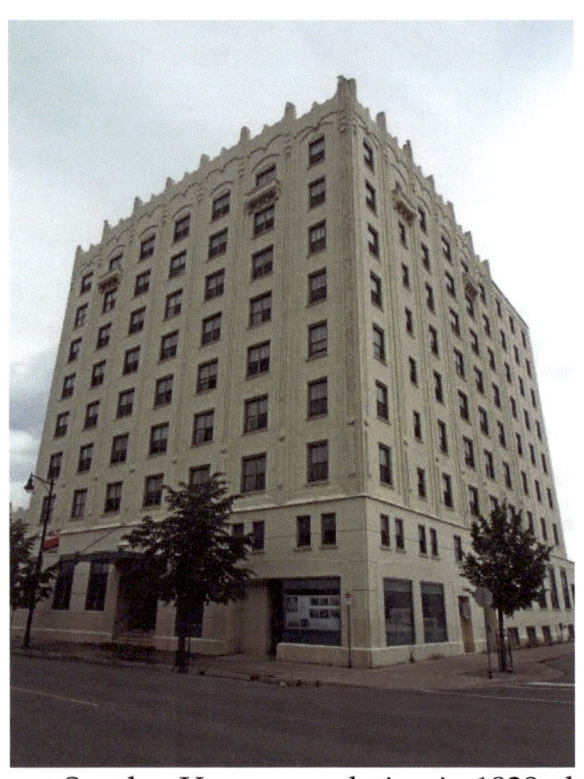

114 May Street South – Upon completion in 1929, the Royal Edward Arms hotel had 105 rooms, each furnished with a bath and there were an additional twenty-one simple rooms which were available for day rental. The dining room seated 150 people and the kitchen was well equipped to deal with busy dinner hours, with a dishwasher capable of washing 7,000 dishes per hour, a forty-gallon soup kettle and an eight-gallon coffee urn. A large ball room, a convention hall and a banquet hall were also features of the lavish hotel. The Royal Edward Arms was a successfully run hotel for many years. Many notable people spent nights at the hotel, with perhaps the most memorable visit being from the Royal Family; Queen Elizabeth II visited with Prince Charles in the 1950s and although they didn't spend the night, they did rent a day room. - Thunder Bay Book 4

In the 1980s the hotel was converted to apartments. It is in the Art Deco style. Although the exterior has a stucco or plaster look to it especially with the decorative work, the entire building is concrete. Slipform Construction technique is a sliding-form construction method of pouring vertical concrete structures. It begins with the construction of a fixed-diameter form on top of a foundation, with a back-up support and bracing system to ensure that the form maintains its shape during movement. Inside and outside forms create the cavity of the wall, and inside this cavity, reinforcing steel is tied together vertically and horizontally to reinforce the concrete wall. The form is then connected to jack rods with hydraulic jacks, which automatically move the form vertically in minute increments as the concrete is being poured. Once pouring begins, it continues until the top of the structure is reached, allowing for a large poured concrete structure. This method of construction is typically used on large-scale storage silos and other vertical concrete structures, such as elevator cores and batch houses. - Thunder Bay Book 4

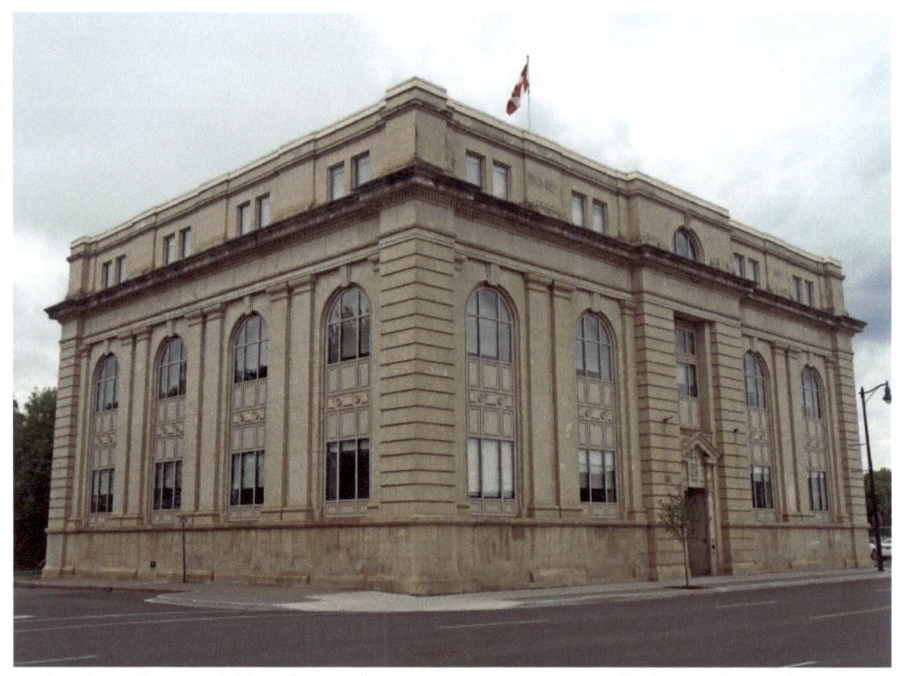

201 May Street North – The Revenue Canada Building is associated with the federal government's expansion of services into smaller communities, and with its provision of well designed, up-to-date facilities. It was built from 1913-1916 when Fort William was one of the world's largest grain-handling ports and a major trade and transportation point and railway terminal. The construction of the building reflects the unprecedented prosperity and optimism of the early twentieth century as well as the expansion of east-west trade and the economic importance of customs activities. The Revenue Canada Building is an example of Beaux-Arts Classicism. This style was commonly used by the Department of Public Works for public institutions in the early twentieth century. The building's good craftsmanship and materials are demonstrated in its use of pale limestone veneer and granite accents on the two principal elevations and in the masonry details. - Thunder Bay Book 4

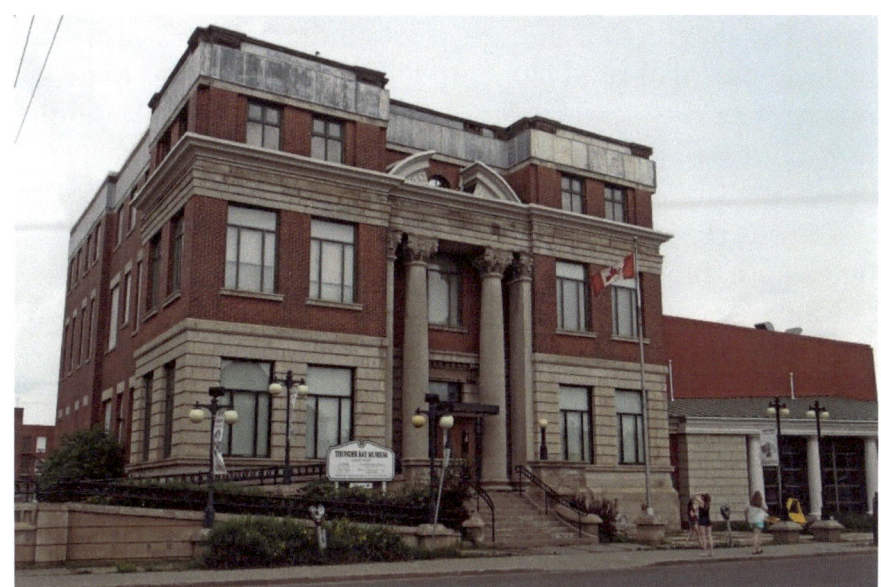

425 Donald Street East – Thunder Bay Museum - The Police Station and Court House was built in 1912. It is an example of the Edwardian Classical style of architecture. It had enough space for a Court room, separate cell blocks for men, women and juveniles, law clerk and magistrate offices as well as a public hall for meetings. A wide flight of curving stone stairs surrounded by a solid, stepped stone parapet leads to an imposing portico. Subdivided into three sections, the central portion of the façade is recessed and framed by two massive columns. The free standing columns rise two stories and are accented by two pilasters that are attached to the façade wall on both sides of the entrance. The placement of these pilasters gives the impression that there are four columns instead of two, creating an interesting optical illusion. The pilasters are also crowned by carved acanthus leaves and small volutes. The tapered columns are adorned by Roman Corinthian capitals. The columns support a massive moulded architrave which extends across the façade; over the entrance is a pediment with a bull's eye window.

The date 1910 is in high relief on the broken pediment. The façade is rusticated stone up to the 2nd floor and the remainder of the façade is faced with Milton brick. Although the windows of the upper portion of the façade have been altered, the stone sills and lintels remain intact. The old police station was renovated to house the Thunder Bay Museum. The major exhibits of the Museum, which opened in 1997, have ample space as additions have been made to the already fair-sized structure. - Thunder Bay Book 4

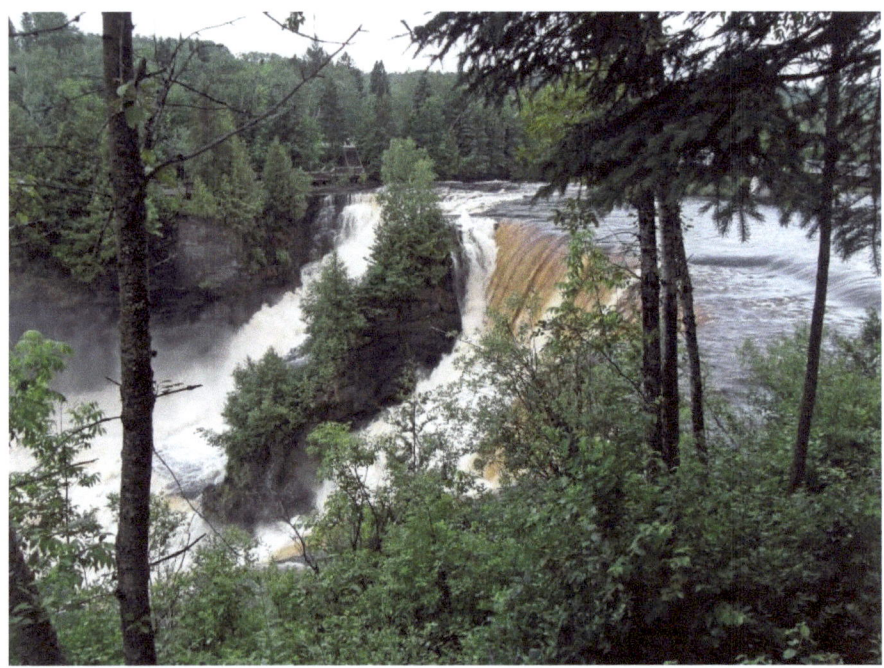

Kakabeka Falls is a waterfall on the Kaministiquia River located thirty kilometers (nineteen miles) west of the city of Thunder Bay. The falls have a drop of forty meters (one hundred and thirty feet), cascading into a gorge. The name "Kakabeka" comes from the Ojibwe word meaning "waterfall over a cliff". - Thunder Bay Book 4

Sudbury, Ontario in Colour Photos – My Top 4 Picks

      Greater Sudbury is the largest city in Northern Ontario. Sudbury was founded in 1883 following the discovery of nickel ore during the construction of the transcontinental railway. The people live in an urban core and many smaller communities scattered around three hundred lakes and among hills of rock blackened by smelting activity. Mining and related industries dominated the economy for much of the twentieth century. The two major mining companies which shaped the history of Sudbury were Inco, now Vale Limited, which employed more than 25% of the population by the 1970s, and Falconbridge, now Glencore. Sudbury has since expanded from its resource-based economy to emerge as the major retail, economic, health and educational centre for North-eastern Ontario.

      The city recovered from the Great Depression much more quickly than almost any other city in North America due to increased demand for nickel in the 1930s. Sudbury was the fastest-growing city and one of the wealthiest cities in Canada for most of the decade. Many of the city's social problems in the Great Depression era were caused by the difficulty in keeping up with all of the new infrastructure demands created by rapid growth. Employed mineworkers sometimes ended up living in boarding houses or makeshift shanty towns because demand for new housing was rising faster than supply.

The open coke beds used in the early to mid-twentieth century and logging for fuel resulted in almost a total loss of native vegetation in the area. Consequently, the terrain was made up of exposed rocky outcrops permanently stained charcoal black, first by the air pollution from the roasting yards. Acid rain added more staining, in a layer that penetrates up to three inches into the once pink-grey granite.

The construction of the Inco Super stack in 1972 dispersed sulphuric acid through the air over a much wider area, reducing the acidity of local precipitation. This enabled the city to begin an environmental recovery program. In the late 1970s, private and public interests combined to establish a "regreening" effort. Lime was spread over the charred soil by hand and by aircraft. Seeds of wild grasses and other vegetation were also spread. More than nine million new trees have been planted in the city.

Sudbury's pentlandite, pyrite and pyrrhotite ores contain profitable amounts of many elements — primarily nickel and copper, but also platinum, palladium and other valuable metals.

There are many details and pictures about rocks and their formation in the book on Sudbury.

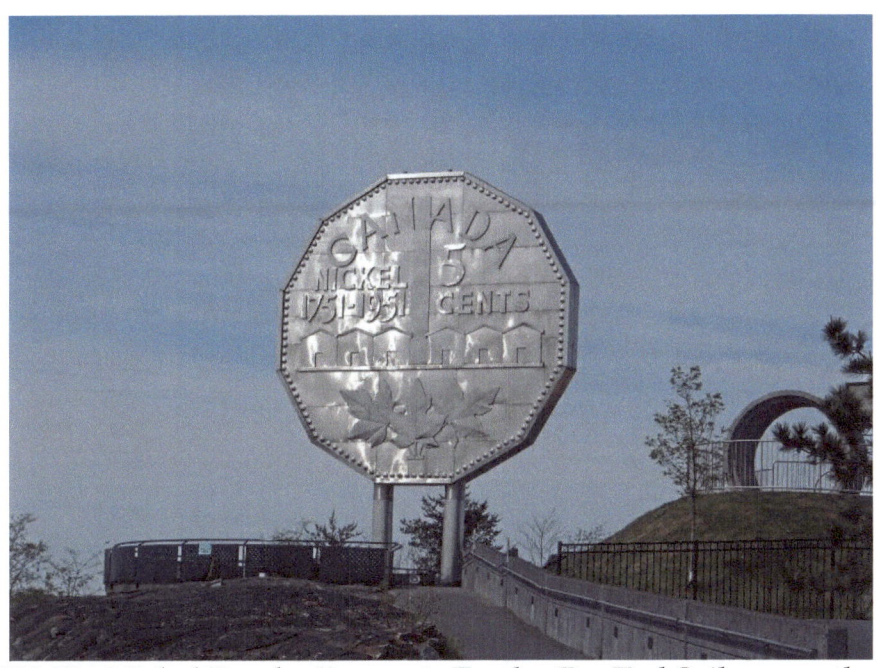

122 Big Nickel Road – Dynamic Earth - Dr. Ted Szilva was the creator of the Canadian Centennial Numismatic Park which opened on July 22, 1964. Ted spearheaded the creation of the Big Nickel and the original Big Nickel mine on the Dynamic Earth site. Today, the Big Nickel is an icon synonymous with Sudbury, the nickel capital of the world. In 1949 the Bank of Canada launched a nationwide contest for the design of the 1951 five-cent coin to mark the bicentennial of the chemical isolation of nickel by the Swedish chemist Baron Axel Frederic Cronstedt. The Big Nickel is a replica of this commemorative 12-sided coin designed by Stephen Trenka. The obverse features King George VI who was the monarch at the time. The reverse features a stylized nickel refinery with one large smokestack. It weighs almost 13,000 kilograms and is nine meters in diameter.

Scientists and residents of Greater Sudbury work hand in hand to innovate and implement new strategies to re-green the community. The City of Greater Sudbury is a world leader in reclamation of environmentally impacted landscapes. The main components of Sudbury's ore are nickel, copper and sulphur. Early methods of smelting released a lot of sulphur dioxide gas (SO_2) into the atmosphere. Since the early 1970s, SO_2 has been greatly reduced which has fostered ecological recovery. In 2015, healthy, reproducing small mouth bass returned to Sudbury's Clearwater Lake which is slowly recovering from acidification.

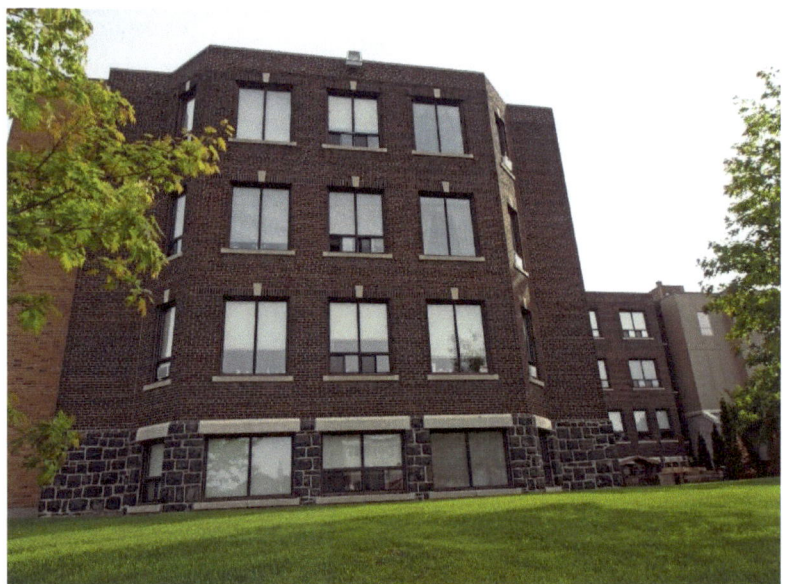

20 Ste. Anne Road – St. Joseph's Hospital - Original building 1898, Surgical Ward added 1914, 1927 modern laundry added, 1928 new heating plant with a long connecting underground tunnel. In 1975 the Hospital was closed. Partially demolished, the remaining portion is now operating as Red Oak Villa retirement home.

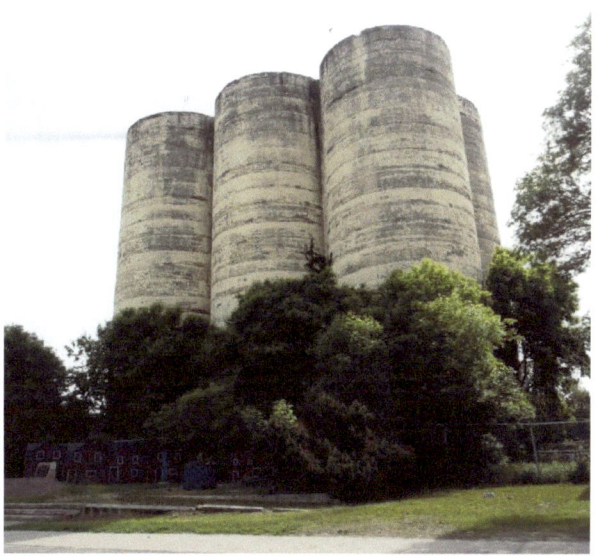

Notre Dame Avenue - Flour Mill Silos

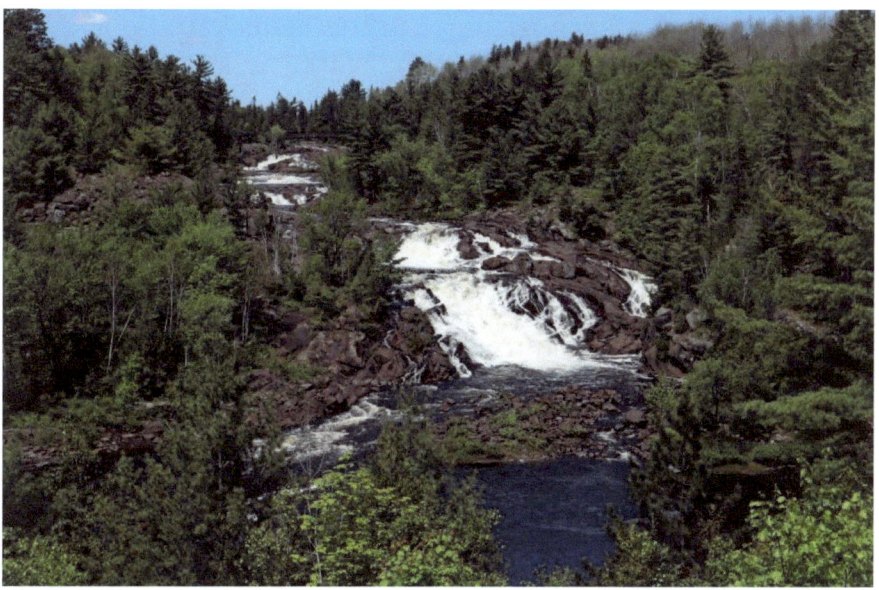

High Falls on the Onaping River drops 46 meters (150 feet) – In 1953 A.Y. Jackson, one of the founding members of the Group of Seven, painted "Spring on the Onaping River."

North Bay, Ontario in Colour Photos – My Top 11 Picks

North Bay is a city in Northeastern Ontario about 330 kilometers (210 miles) north of Toronto. It differs in geography from Southern Ontario because North Bay is situated on the Canadian Shield which results in a more rugged landscape. North Bay straddles both the Ottawa River watershed to the east and the Great Lakes Basin to the west. The city's urban core is located between Lake Nipissing and the smaller Trout Lake.

In 1882, John Ferguson decided that the north bay of Lake Nipissing was a promising spot for settlement. Apart from Indigenous people, voyageurs and surveyors, there was little activity in the Lake Nipissing area until the arrival of the Canadian Pacific Railway (CPR) in 1882. North Bay was selected as the southern terminus of the Temiskaming and Northern Ontario Railway (T&NO) in 1902 when the Ross government took the bold move to establish a development road to serve the Haileybury settlement. During construction of the T&NO, silver was discovered at Cobalt and started a mining frenzy in the northern part of the province that continued for many years. The Canadian Northern Railway was built to North Bay in 1913.

North Bay grew through a strong lumbering sector, mining and the three railways in the early days.

Born in France about 1598, Jean Nicolet, explorer, fur trader, and interpreter came to Canada in 1618. Under orders from Samuel de Champlain, he spent the following two years with the Algonquins of Allumette Island. He was then sent to the Nipissing Indians of this area and dwelt among them for at least eight years, learning their language, adopting their customs, and strengthening their alliance with the French. Nicolet is credited with the discovery of Lake Michigan which he explored as far south as the head of Green Bay in 1634. He later settled in Trois Rivieres. He drowned in the St. Lawrence in 1642.

The rivers and lakes of northern Ontario have been highways for travel and commerce for hundreds of years. First nations and European explorers used Lake Nipissing for transporting their furs. When the railroad reached the area in the 1880s, settlers and timber were transported across the lake.

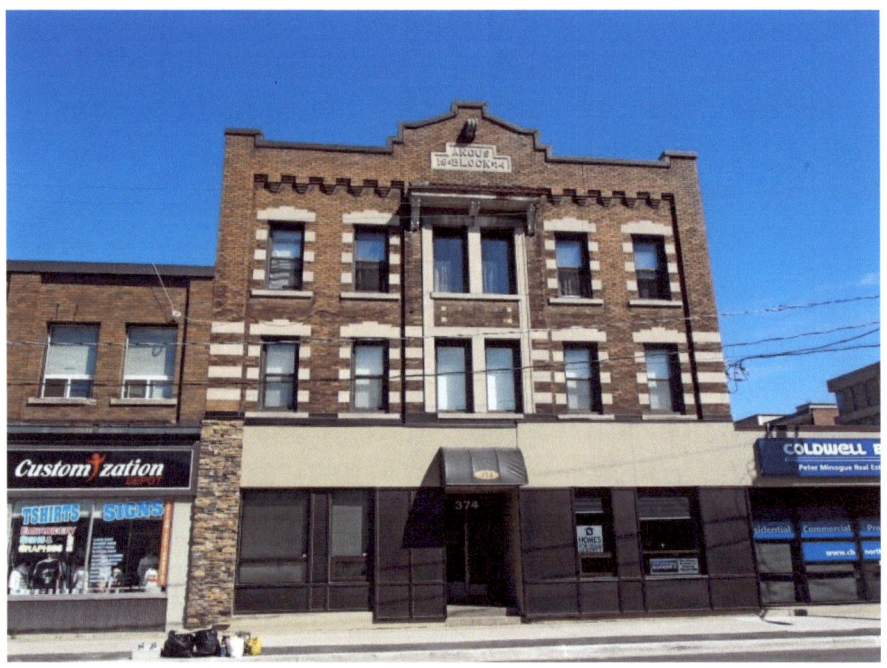

374 Fraser Street – Angus Block – 1914 – This building is noted for its parapet at the roof line and for its highly distinctive white stone window surrounds consisting of stepped lintels, quoined jambs and flat sills. Other notable features include the toothed heading of the in-stepped brick facing and bracketed canopy over the third-floor paired openings. The date stone indicates that H.W. Angus, an early architect in North Bay, was responsible for its design and erection.

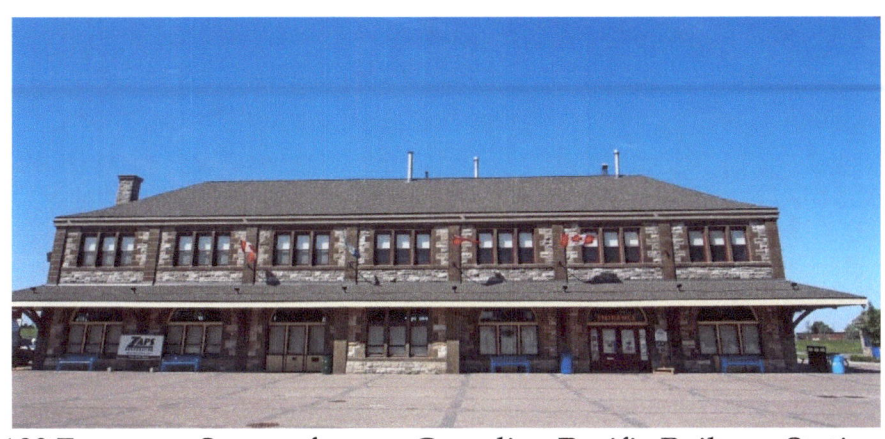

100 Ferguson Street - former Canadian Pacific Railway Station – 1903 - Entry of British Columbia into Confederation in 1871 led to the establishment of the CPR as the initial continental railway linking the country's east and west coasts, completed in 1885. In 1881 the railway located their divisional services and regional headquarters on the shore of Lake Nipissing, where the City of North Bay subsequently sprang up. The stone masonry is of a variegated light beige color of split-faced finish, laid in a random-coursed pattern. The corner and intermittent piers and window surrounds are of a uniform darker brown tone of flat-faced finish, laid in a level course pattern. Most openings at ground floor level are of the Romanesque round-head arched style. A wide bracketed canopy projects on all sides at the second-floor level, offering protection from the weather to passengers, their luggage, and accompanying freight. The Canadian Pacific Railway reached North Bay in 1882 and the area became a crucial junction point between east and west rail traffic.

In 1901, the CPR made North Bay the District Divisional headquarters; repair shops began to dominate the North Bay waterfront. The site eventually housed an eighteen-stall engine house, freight and flour sheds, carpenter and car repair shops, ice houses, a yard office, railway stores, and the engineer booking office. There was also a vast locomotive shop used to repair steam engines. At its peak, the yard could hold two hundred railroad cars and it contained twenty-five miles of track. During the 1940s, four transcontinental trains a day came through the yards. To the west of the main depot was a well-maintained grassy park with numerous flower gardens and trees.

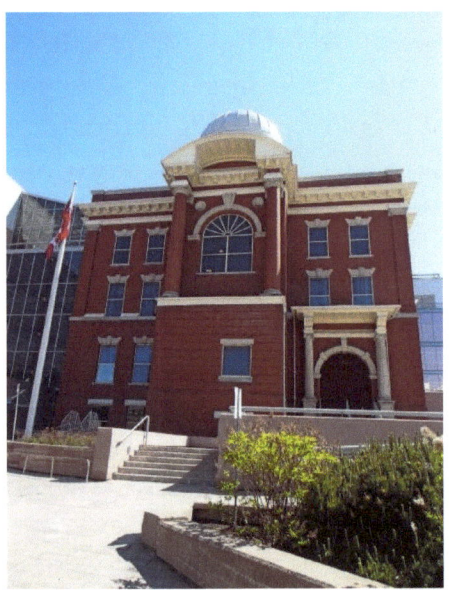

200 First Avenue West - Former Normal School/Teacher's College opened in 1909 with an enrolment of 25 students and continued in operation until 1972. This design is exemplary of the architectural influence of the Edwardian style. The observatory-like dome, the elaborate cornices and the formal entrance are three main characteristics of the building.

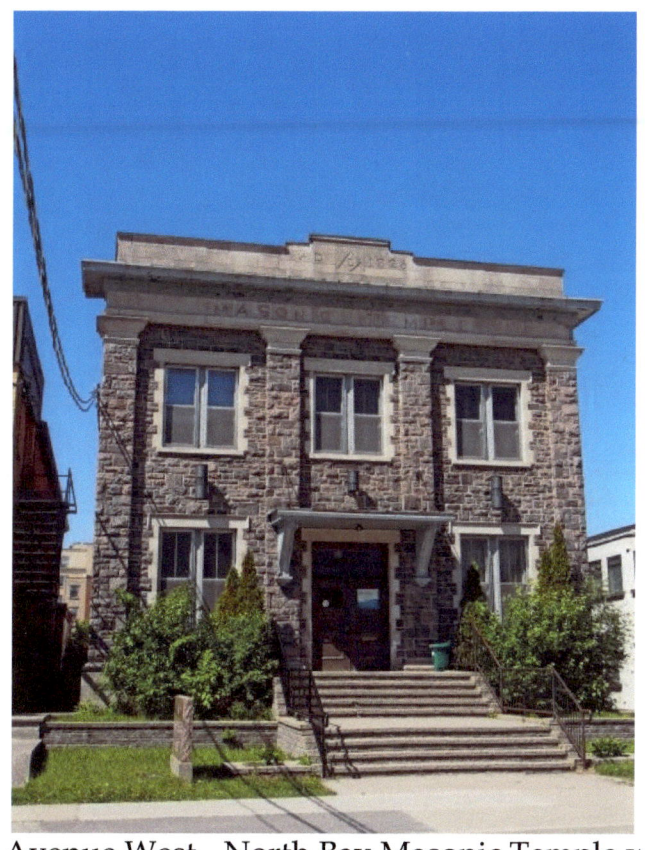

183 First Avenue West - North Bay Masonic Temple was built in 1928 and was first used as a meeting and dance hall. During the Second World War it served as a center for medical examinations of those local residents contemplating military service. The building is neo-classical in style with a symmetrical front façade. The outstanding architectural features of this building include the engaged piers and stepped parapet carried by the entablature. The grand stone entranceway expresses the major function of this structure as an assembly hall.

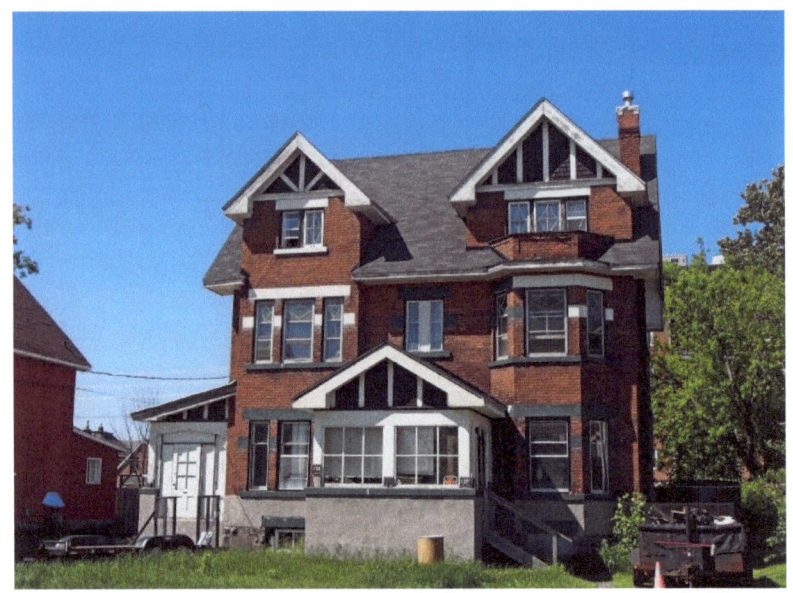

135-137 First Avenue West – 2½-storey bays with Tudor timbering in gables, diamond window panes

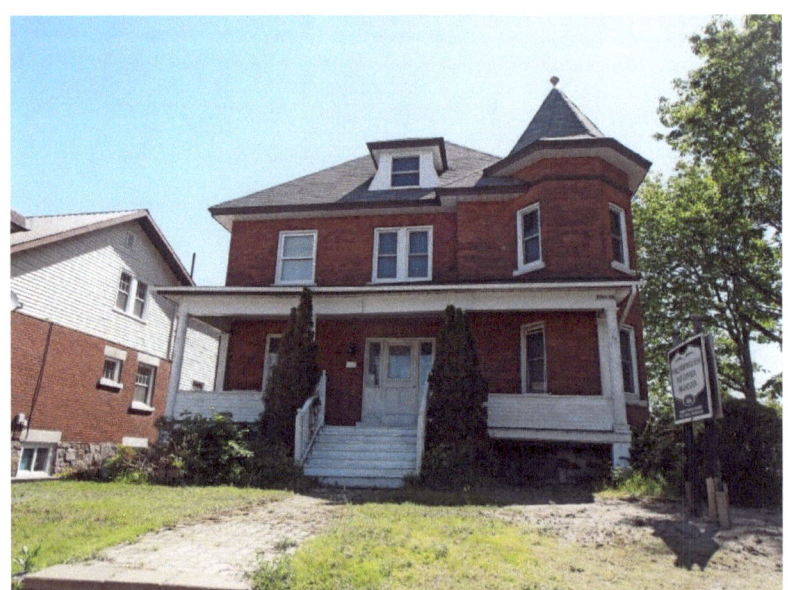

406 McIntyre Street West – two-storey bay with octagonal capped roof, dormer

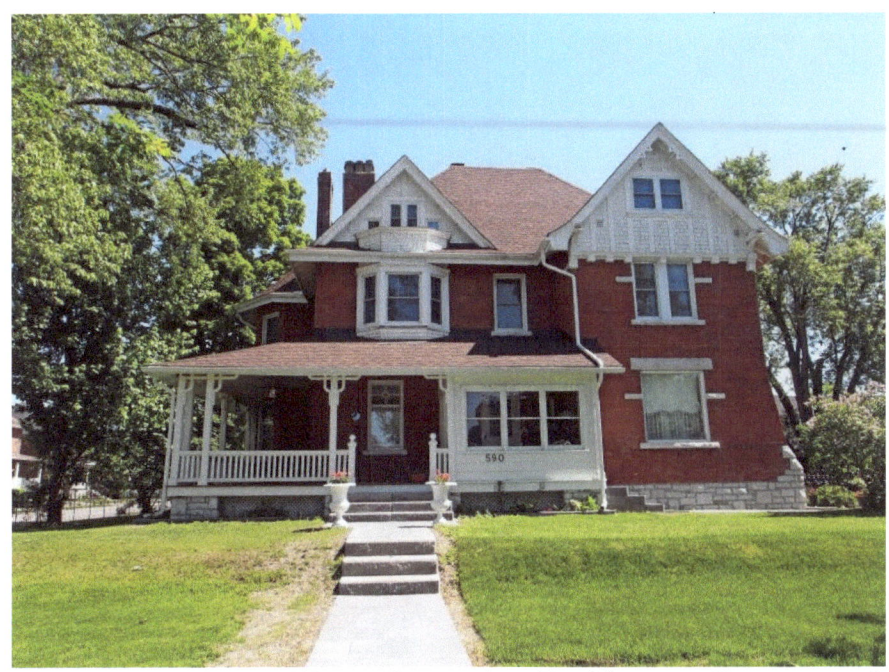

590 McIntyre Street West - Browning Residence - Constructed in 1902, it was originally occupied by Crown Prosecutor A.G. Browning and his family. It is set on a large corner lot at Murray Street, among mature trees. A strong symmetry of the main façade was originally developed in a three-bay roofed front porch at ground floor level leading to the main entry, above which is a second-floor bay window whose structure extends through the main roof eave to form a unique mini-balcony centered on a third-floor windowed gable. This symmetry is offset by a three-story gabled wing on one side, and the wrap-around porch terminating at a corner bay on the Murray Street side.

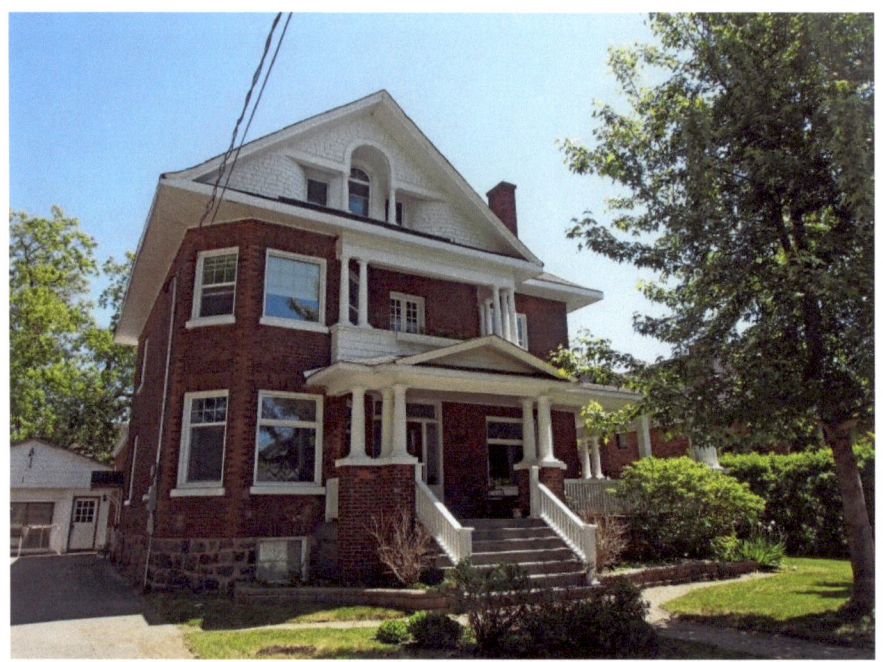

658 McIntyre Street West – The Bourke Residence was built in 1907. The structural, yet decorative columns and the boxed-in triangular pediment over the porch area are strong elements of the design. The two-story bay windows and the wraparound porch are also distinctive. Symmetry is established, centered on the main entrance, in the access stair, the pediment enhanced porch, and the second-floor balcony. The windowed gable at the attic level is centered independently on the main front wing of the L-shaped structure. The home was once the residence of the first Mayor of the City of North Bay, John Bourke.

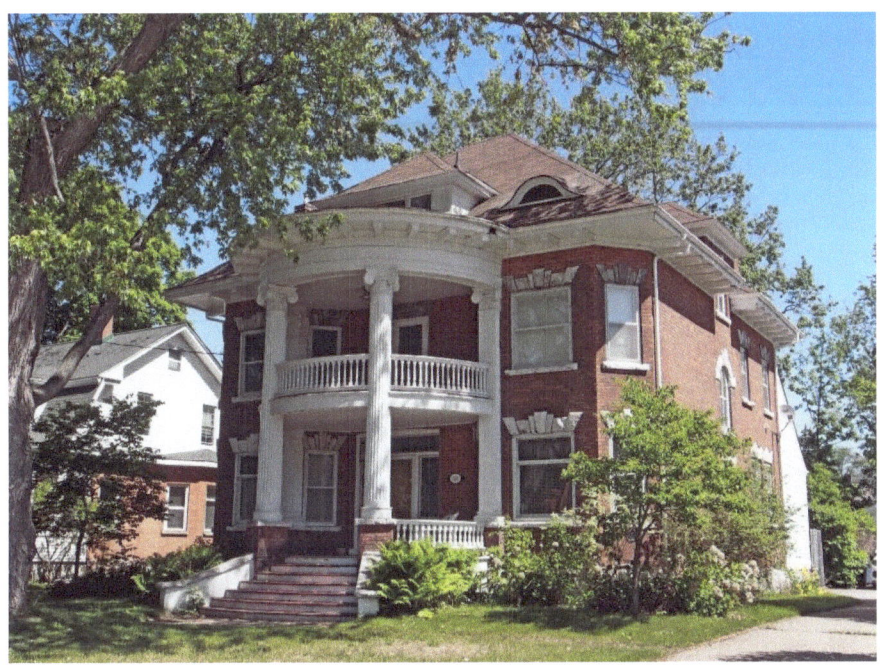

768 McIntyre Street West – The Beamish Residence was constructed in 1907. The two-story front porch is large and has Ionic columns. It has a hipped roof with wave-form dormer windows. A strong symmetry is centered on the two-story wood porch between matched masonry bays. The fanned steps of the main entry are very generous in scale, and thus appropriately related to the proportions of the entire front façade. The front entrance is the only item that is off center. A well-preserved home of majestic stature, it was once the original residence of a local merchant, Mr. Beamish. Mr. Jack Shaw, former North Bay Mayor, also resided here. Mr. Arthur Cavanaugh, former manager of Ontario Northland Railway, lived in this house from 1940-1950.

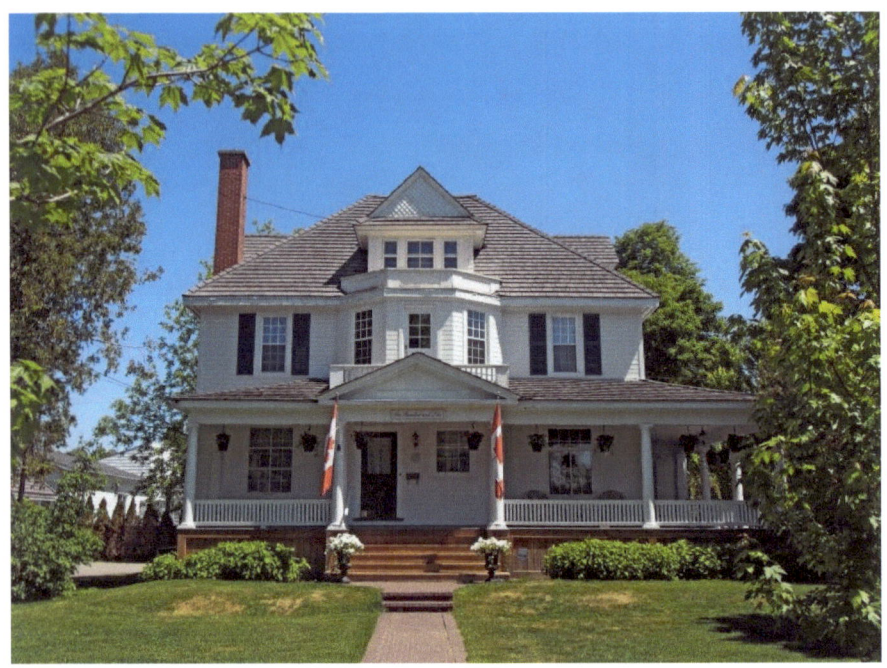

610 Copeland Avenue – The Milne Residence is an impressive home located on an unusually large lot. It was built for William Milne Sr. in the early 1900s. Milne was the owner of Wm. Milne & Sons Lumber Company which was located at the present site of the Ministry of Natural Resources on Trout Lake Road from the early 1900s to 1944. Milne was also a former alderman and Mayor of North Bay in 1909 and 1910. The house is set back on the property. The large side yard housed a tennis court during the first two decades of the house. The exterior is simple, but the structure is reminiscent of the local history of the lumber and crafts industry. The exterior walls are sheathed with shiplap-type wood siding. The roof is sheathed in wood shingles. The veranda, which wraps around the front and side of the home, once extended to the rear of the home as well, but it was later removed.

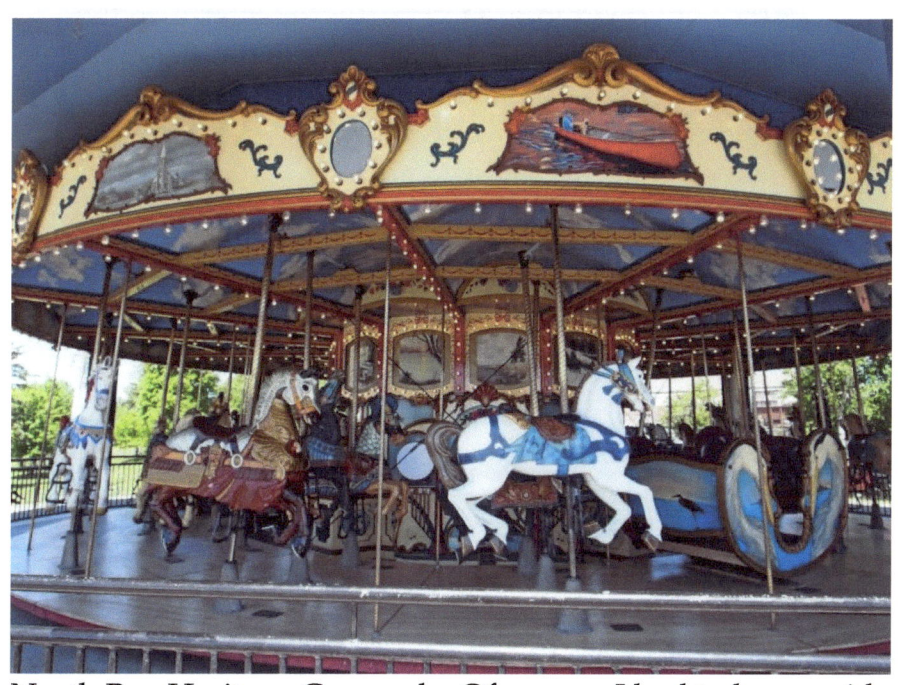

North Bay Heritage Carousel – Of course, I had to have a ride on it while I was there!

Parry Sound, Ontario in Colour Photos – My Top 11 Picks

Parry Sound is a located in northern Ontario on the eastern shore of Parry Sound. It is 160 kilometres (99 miles) south of Sudbury and 225 kilometres (140 miles) north of Toronto. It is a popular cottage country region. It has the world's deepest natural freshwater port.

Muskoka District was named after an Indian Chief, probably Misquuckkey of the Chippawas, who until the treaty of 1815 was lord of this Venetian district of Ontario. While the heavy pine and hardwood forests were still in their primeval beauty, many people including Government agents considered the country was fit for settlement. In 1859 the first land grants were made.

About 1857 James and William Gibson erected a sawmill at the mouth of the Seguin River. William Beatty, with his sons James and William, acquired the mill in 1863, and the following year were granted a licence of occupation for two thousand acres. In addition to lumbering, they laid out a town plot, promoted settlement, opened a store, built a church, constructed roads, and operated boats on Lake Huron and a stage service to Bracebridge. William "Governor" Beatty (1835-1898) lived here and managed the family's enterprises which stimulated the growth of Parry Sound. Incorporated as a town in 1887, it was named in honour of Sir William Edward Parry, noted Arctic explorer.

During the early part of the 20th century, the area was a popular subject for the many scenic art works of Tom Thomson and members of the Group of Seven.

The eastern coast of Georgian Bay where Parry Sound is located is known as the "30,000 Islands" and is considered the world's largest freshwater archipelago. It covers 347,000 hectares of shoreline ecosystem, and over 100 species of animals and plants that are at risk in Canada and Ontario, including unique reptiles and amphibians.

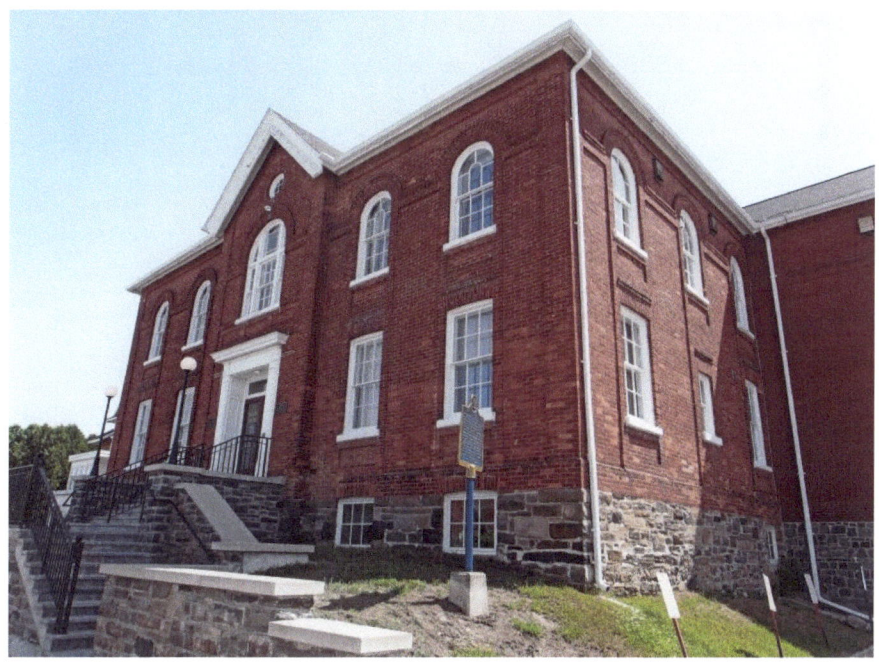

89 James Street – Court House - 1871

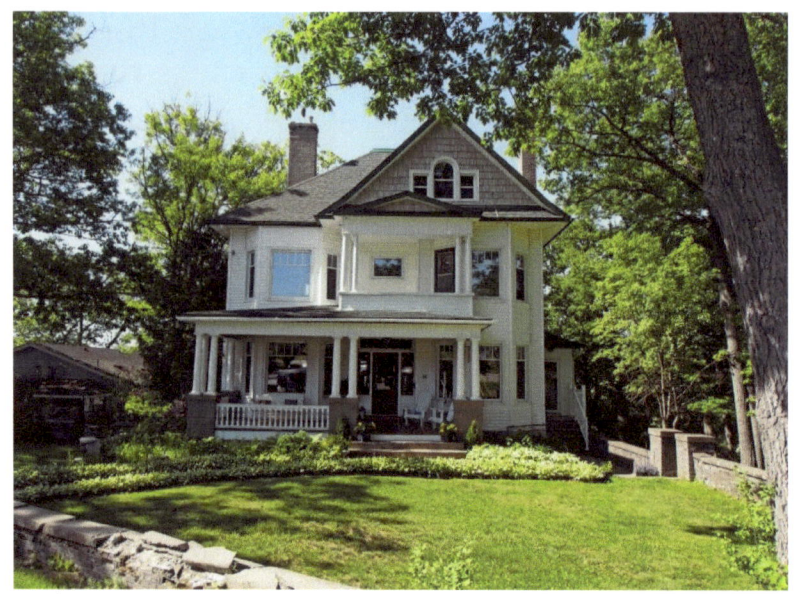

18 Belvedere Avenue – Palladian window in gable, second-floor balcony

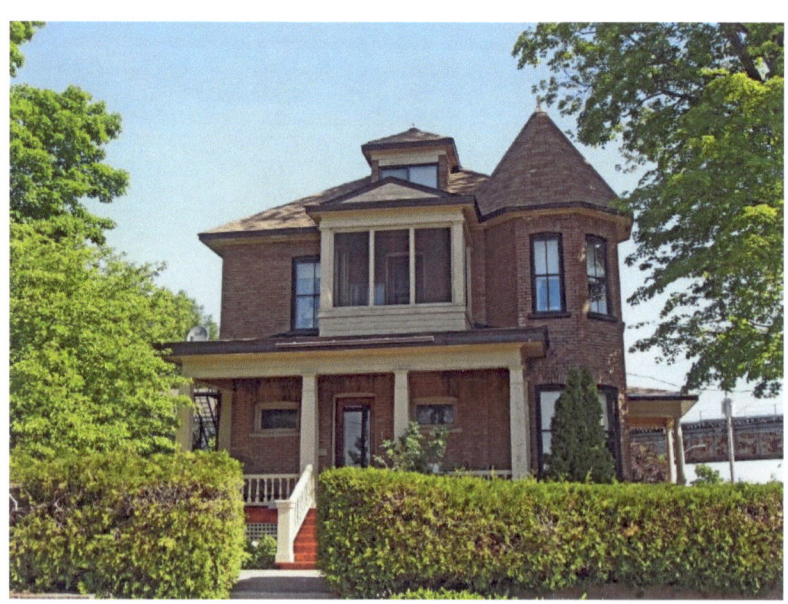

1 Belvedere Avenue – 1907 – two-storey tower, dormer in attic

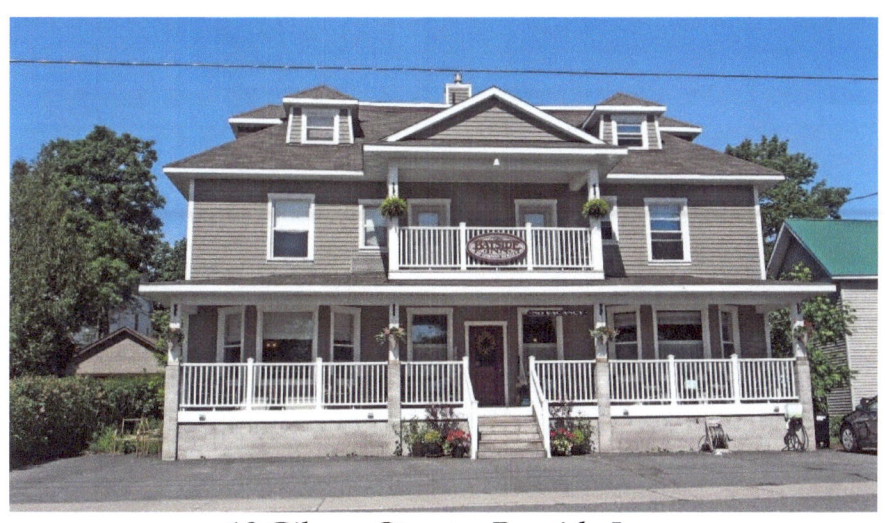

10 Gibson Street – Bayside Inn

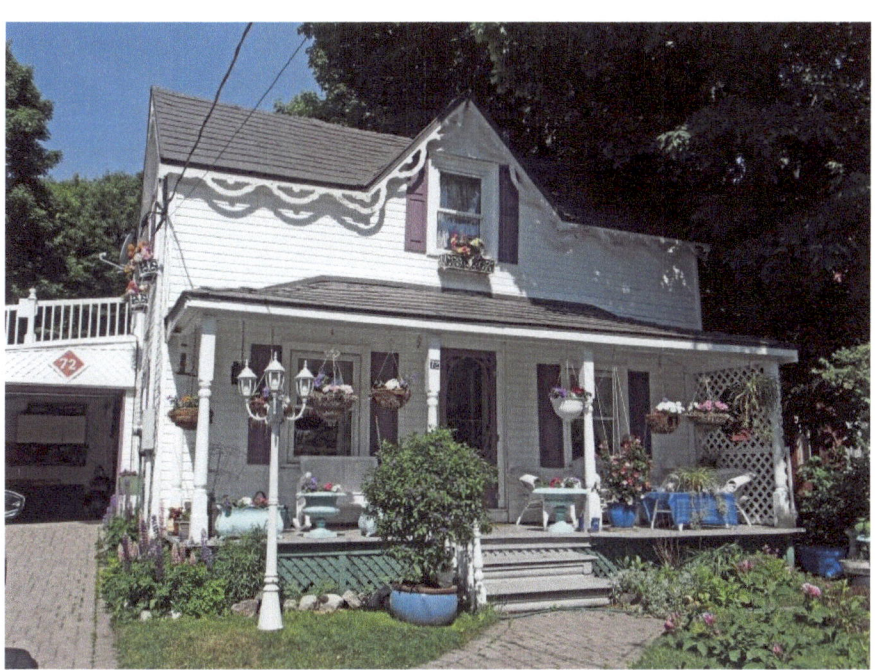

72 Gibson Street – verge board trim – Gerda's Bed and Breakfast

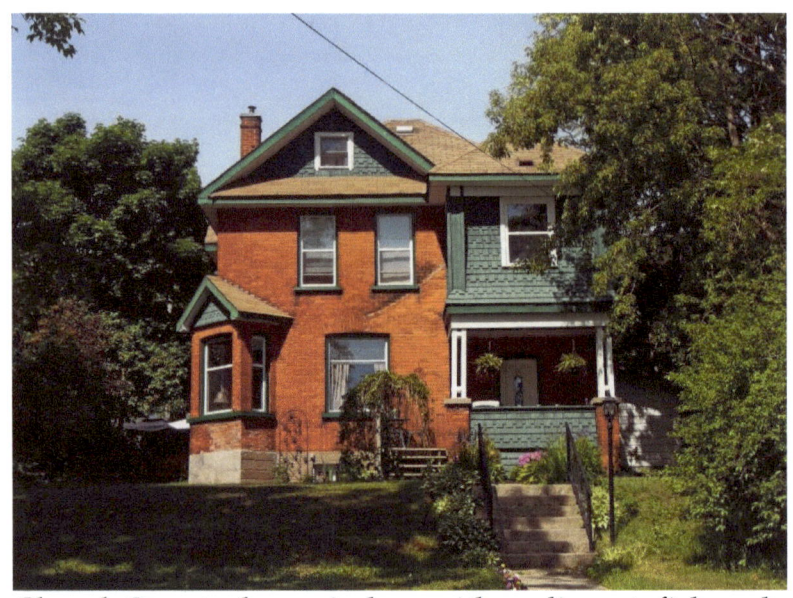

Church Street – bay window with pediment, fish scale patterning

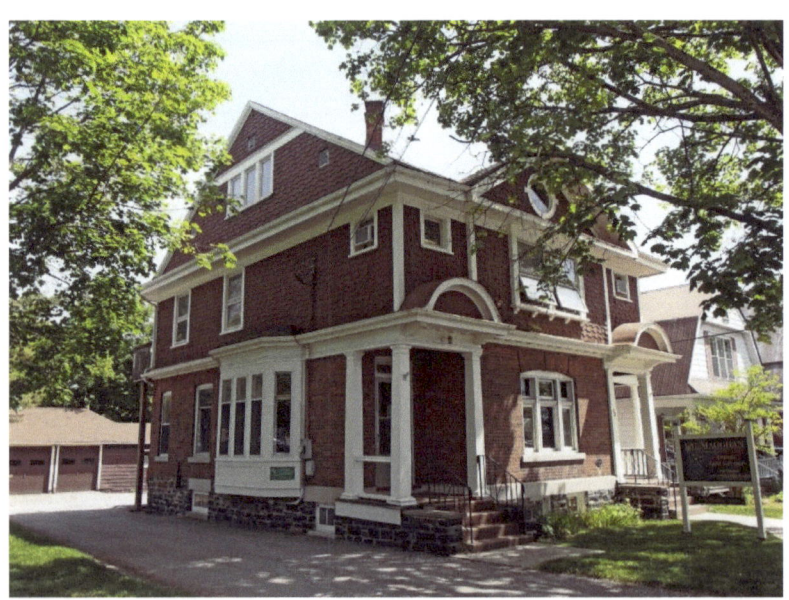

5 McMurray Street – bay window on side, semi-circular pediments

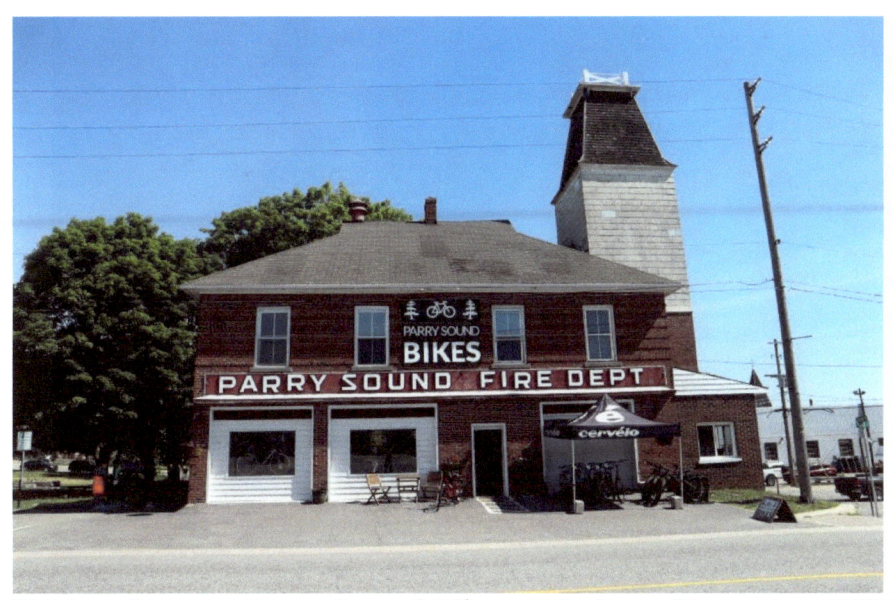

25 Mary Street – Parry Sound Bikes – Heritage Property - 1893

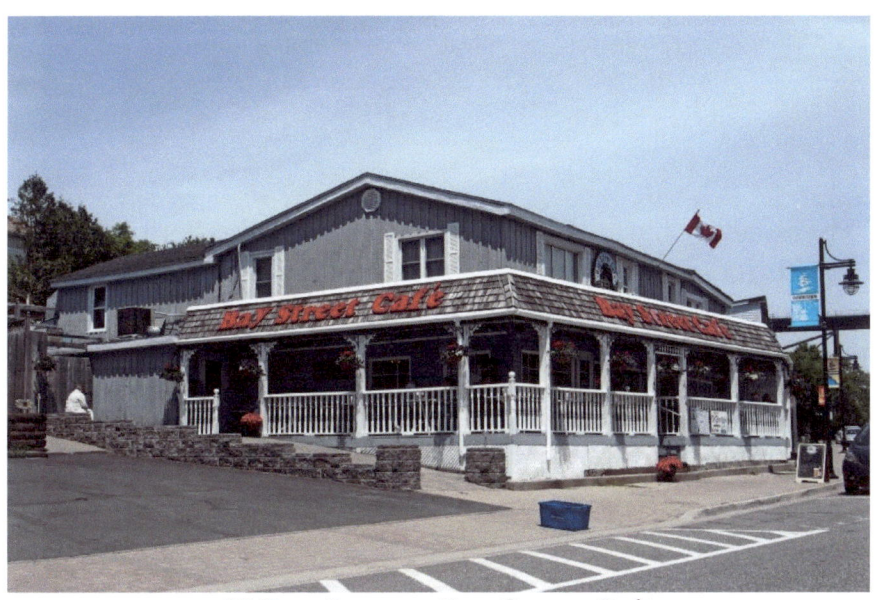

22 Bay Street – Bay Street Café

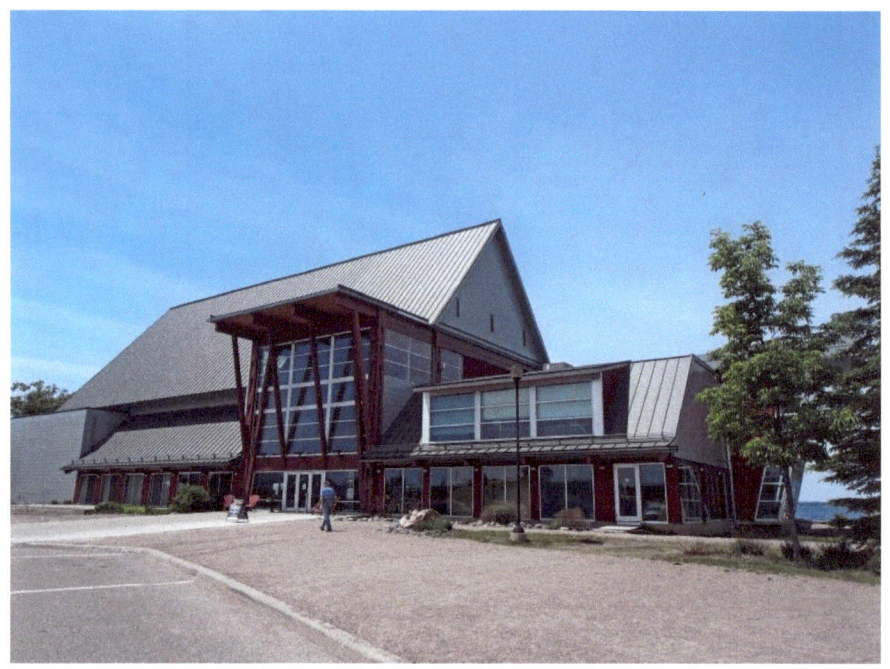

2 Bay Street - Charles W. Stockey Centre for the Performing Arts overlooks Georgian Bay and has a 415 seat acoustically perfect performance hall. The Bobby Orr Hall of Fame is an interactive sports heritage museum paying tribute to hometown hockey legend, Bobby Orr, and other exceptional athletes with connections to Parry Sound.

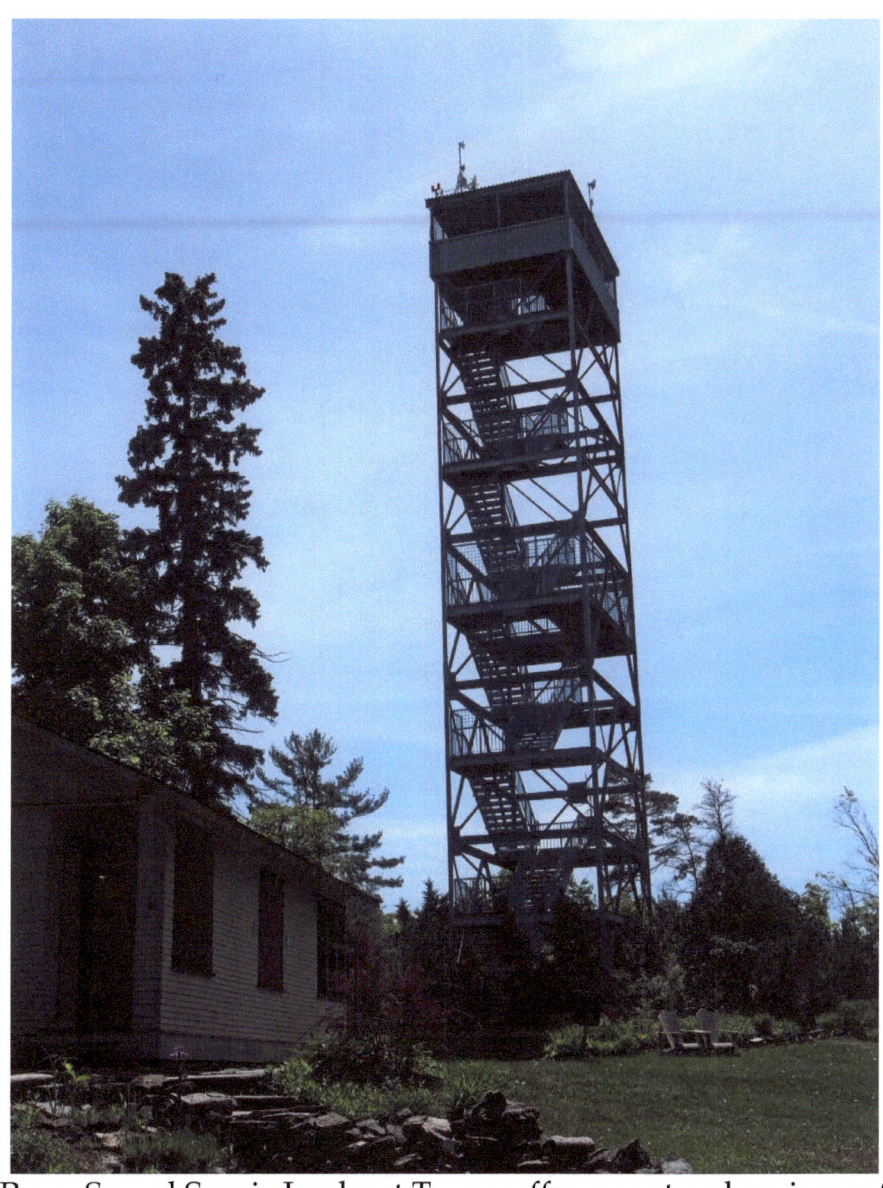

Parry Sound Scenic Lookout Tower offers spectacular views of the harbor and Georgian Bay. Climb 30 meters up a historic fire observation tower to enjoy a spectacular 360 view of Parry Sound.

Other Books by Barbara Raue

Coins of Gold
Arrows, Indians and Love
The Life and Times of Barbara
The Cromwell Family Book
Laura Secord Discovered
Daddy Where Are You?

Montana Series
Book 1: Montana Dream
Book 2: Life on the Montana Frontier
Book 3: Montana to Boston and Back
Book 4: Montana Sons Go to War
Book 5: Montana Sons Return from War

Book 1: Rite of Passage
Book 2: Rite of Marriage

© 2019 by Barbara Raue - All the photos in this book have been taken with my cameras. I own the rights to them.

Barbara is The Authority on Saving Our History One Photo at a Time. She is pursuing her interest in photography and architecture by preserving a record through photos of old buildings from the 1800s and 1900s with their unique architecture. Enjoy the beautiful architecture in the comfort of your living room. Dream about what it was like in those by-gone days. Dream about what it was like to live in a mansion like one of those in this book.

Barbara Raue, a wife, mother and grandmother, is an avid reader and writer. She has researched and compiled several family histories. In 2010, Barbara published her book "Coins of Gold," which celebrates the courageous life of her mother, May Todd. Barbara's second book is a historical fiction "Arrows, Indians and Love" which takes place in Boonesborough, Kentucky during the time of Daniel Boone. In 2013, Barbara published *The Cromwell Family Book* in which she traces her ancestry generations back into Great Britain. Her second novel is called *Laura Secord Discovered,* in which the story of Laura's service during the War of 1812 is shared. Barbara's memoir is titled *Daddy Where Are You?* It tells of her life growing up without a father. Five novels in the Montana Series have been published, *Montana Dream, Life on the Montana Frontier, Montana to Boston and Back, Montana Sons Go to War,* and *Montana Sons Return from War.*

This is a link to Barbara's website to view all of her books
http://barbararaue.ca

www.ingramcontent.com/pod-product-compliance
Lightning Source LLC
Chambersburg PA
CBHW040227220526
45473CB00001B/146